Chapels of the Rough Bounds:

Morar, Knoydart, Arisaig, Moidart

Alasdair Roberts

First published in 2015 by
Mallaig Heritage Centre
Station Road
Mallaig
Inverness-shire
PH41 4PY

www.mallaigheritage.org.uk

ISBN 978 0 9565853 5 6

Contents

Acknowledgements

The name of the late Paul Galbraith, formerly of Bracara in Morar, appears many times in what follows. Without his *Blessed Morar* this book could hardly have been written. These others have also helped in various ways: Gordon Barr, Ronald Black, Molly Buchanan, Fr. Joseph Calleja, Jean Cameron, Hugh Cheape, Marlene MacDonald Cheng, John Dye, Sandra Evans, Rob Fairley, Jean-Didier Hache, Fr. Michael Hutson, Jean Lawson, Allan MacDonald, Elizabeth MacDonald, Fr. Michael MacDonald, Mgr. Roddie MacDonald, Mary MacDonell, Brian Murray, Malcolm Poole, Tearlach MacFarlane, Denis Rixson, Tim Roberton, Deirdre Roberts, Martin Roberts, Donald William Stewart, Iain Thornber, Fr. Tony Wood, John Watts, Mgr Thomas Wynne.

I am grateful to the following for kindly permitting me to use photographs and illustrations: Fr. Joseph Calleja, Matt and Sam Humphrey, Jean Lawson, Alexander Mathieson, Denis Rixson, Fr. Tony Wood.

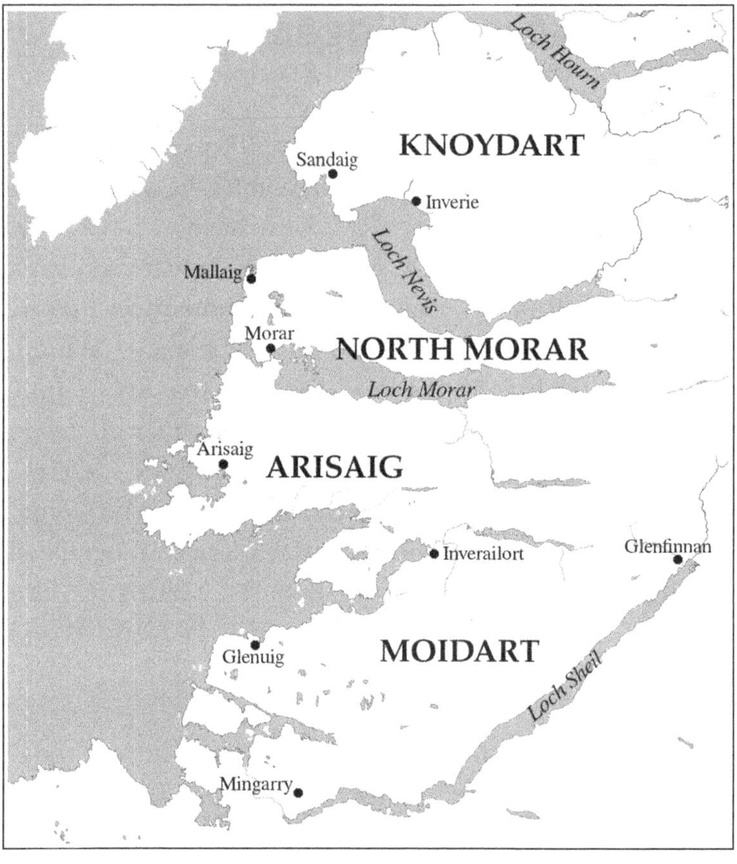

THE 'ROUGH BOUNDS'

Introduction

Morar is in the roughest part of four linked West Highland districts. Our part of the north shore of Loch Morar goes by the name of Bracara. Breac recalls Alan Breck Stewart in Stevenson's *Kidnapped*, so called because of his smallpox scars. The scattered stones on the hillside are reminiscent of that. Garbh means rough. The two words are linked as Breckgarvruick and Breckgarvnantor in an eighteenth century estate rental: Rocky Bracara for added emphasis and Bracara of the Hill. The loch is the deepest fresh-water lake in Britain and one of the deepest in Europe. North and South Morar, which extend twelve miles due east to the head of the loch, lie at the heart of the *Garbh Chriochan*, the Rough Bounds between Knoydart and Moidart.

Knoydart, which has been described as Britain's last wilderness, is a broad peninsula between two sea lochs. There is no road in beyond the head of Loch Hourn, which is reached by way of Loch Garry and Loch Quoich. The motorist's descent to Loch Hourn (the name comes from *iutharn* meaning hellish) is through a remarkable bleak and stony moonscape. Thereafter the map's straight track along the loch side gives no idea of the rising and falling challenge of the walk into Knoydart. A Catholic bishop described it as worse than anything he had experienced in the Alps.

However there is easy access to Knoydart by boat from the rail terminus at Mallaig. The recent upgrading of a hazardous road from Fort William, hitherto single-track over long stretches, has resulted in what feels like motorway driving. The Road to the Isles (*Rathad nan Eilean*) can now be enjoyed. At Lochailort there is a choice between turning south for Moidart or continuing north by way of Arisaig and Morar. 'The remotest pub on the British mainland' – The Old Forge at Inverie in Knoydart - can be reached without difficulty. A short crossing of Loch Nevis (*neamhaidh* or heavenly) brings passengers to shore. Beside the new pier cars are landed from time to time but there are only seven miles of road in Knoydart.

Before there were wheeled vehicles of any kind in the Rough Bounds, a government agent described the whole awesome region as 'the Highlands of the Highlands'. Morar was equally hard to reach by land. When General Wade and his construction teams reached Lochaber, the military road took a wide curve round the area between Fort William and the Bernera barracks at Kirkton of Glenelg.

Knoydart and North Morar were associated with the MacDonell chiefs of Glengarry. The MacDonalds of Morar – really South Morar - looked towards the Captain of Clanranald, a chief whose territory included lands in Arisaig and Moidart. Clanranald also held parts of the Small Isles and the Outer Hebrides. The two spellings 'MacDonald' and 'MacDonell' were used indifferently in eighteenth century documents, with *Mhic Dhomhnaill* or 'son of Donald' the unwritten down-the-nose origin of both. Arisaig and Moidart to the south were both in Clanranald country, with Castle Tioram the mainland base matching residences of the clan chief in Benbecula and South Uist.

Taking a final overview of the Rough Bounds, there are six sea lochs from north to south and two significant freshwater ones. Loch Morar is noted for its extreme depth and the large aquatic beasts which occasionally surface. Loch Shiel extends from the Green Isle of ancient burials to Glenfinnan, where the Stuart standard was raised in 1745. Five MacDonald brothers of Kinlochmoidart (Highland gentlemen of the 'tacksman' class) came out in support of Prince Charles Edward Stuart and suffered for it. After the final defeat at Culloden, houses great and small were burned between Knoydart and Moidart.

The whole area was Catholic, hence the interest in chapels. In Victorian times senior clergy of the Roman Catholic Church in Scotland tried to replace 'chapel' with 'church' but the older usage persisted – not least in the immigrant Irish communities of central Scotland. The largest building to be considered here appears on the map showing Arisaig village as St Mary's Chapel. Most of them, however, are humble enough.

So much for geography. On a personal level, my wife Deirdre and I came to live in Morar twenty years ago. For most of that time she has reared unusual breeds of sheep on an eight-acre croft, putting her degree in agriculture to good use. That phase ended when we moved to a new house on the other side of the road. It is a spectacular site above Loch Morar. The road is a crumbling single-track which ends a little further on, but a ten-minute drive takes us into Mallaig with its shops, restaurants and tourist outlets. Deirdre has a craft shed where she cards, spins, dyes and weaves wool for

EILEAN BAN, LOCH MORAR

sale. I write Highland history. One of its more dramatic episodes, at the end of the 1745 Jacobite Rising and described in a *Scots Magazine* of the time, describes government troops making a first entry to the Rough Bounds:

'Having apprehended several of the rebels in those parts they learned from them that Lord Lovat, with his servants and a guard of well-armed and resolute men, had retired into an island in Loch Morar, a fresh-water lake twelve miles in length and somewhat more than a mile from the west sea-coast. In this pleasant little island his Lordship lived with MacDonald of Morar the proprietor of it, his brother Bishop Hugh MacDonald the Pope's Apostolical Vicar of Scotland, one Dr MacDonald, and several others of that rebellious family. Here they deemed themselves perfectly secure, having for that end brought all the boats on the lake to their island; never once suspecting the possibility of His Majesty's forces being able to bring any boats from the sea, over land to this lake, to disturb their secure retreat. But they soon found themselves woefully mistaken . . .

'The King's ships having sailed round to that part of the coast where their boats had little more than a mile to be carried overland to the lake (the brook that runs from that lake to the sea near that place being too small for navigation) the rebels immediately lost all courage upon observing the men-of-war's boats moving overland towards the lake, and suddenly taking to their own boats they rowed up the lake with the utmost precipitation. . . All the rebel gentry, MacDonalds, escaped into the mountains excepting the before-named Dr MacDonald whom our people apprehended and brought back to the island, together with the boats of those rebels. Here they found the before-named Bishop's house and chapel which the sailors quickly gutted and demolished, merrily adorning themselves with the spoils of the chapel.'

☩

1 - INVERBEG AT LOCH MORAR

Soon after we came to Morar local historian Paul Galbraith took us to the site of the ruined chapel at Inverbeg. *Inbhir Beag* (the little river-mouth) is a ten-minute walk along the loch side from where the Bracara road ends. We were back at Inverbeg in August 1999 along with forty worshippers led by the musical priest Fr Michael Hutson to that year's Holy Site. As on the sandy white island of *Eilean Bàn* which has just featured, we prayed for priests of former days and in particular for Ranald MacDonell who had the chapel raised.

Before that he was an itinerant priest living with one family after another and catechising children as he went. Sometimes people gathered for worship in a barn or *tigh phìobuill* (house of the people) as at Romasaig further east – another pilgrimage Holy Site. Rain swept in from the loch as we huddled against the wall, and two golf umbrellas sheltered the card table which served as an altar. There was singing in English, Gaelic and Latin. I played *Regina Caeli* on the pipes as I had done earlier that summer while in St Peter's Square with

Morar pilgrims. Then sunshine broke through, and our local pilgrimage became a picnic.

Another picnic began the process of restoration. Three years later I returned with grandsons Thomas, Calum and Lewis to fry sausages in the collapsing north-east corner. Walls were scrambled over while I set about pulling up bracken so that we could sit round the fire. The bracken was taller than the boys and well rooted. I cut my hand and wrapped a handkerchief round the wound, later displaying

CHAPEL WALLS AT INVERBEG

'The Bloody Flag of Inverbeg' for their entertainment. What began as a picnic became a project, with bracken removed from inside and outside the walls over a period of months. Fishermen on the loch could now see the place, and walkers between Bracara and Tarbert no longer passed by unawares. Then reports came back of other people's grandchildren damaging the walls.

The North and South Morar Field Club was formed about this time for the sake of walks and talks. Having come across a cache of letters addressed to Inverbeg, I gave a talk in the Morar Hotel on the priest who served the area for sixty years: *Maighstir Raonall Mac Domhnaill*. There was also a walk to the site. An illustrated brochure showed how the thatched roof would have drained into the middle, where there was rubble between inner and outer walls. Six-inch Ordnance Survey maps showed how what Paul Galbraith called the 'long chapel' became a sheep fank, and then acquired an extension to make the building L-shaped. In order to confine the animals a large window in the west gable, and a small one facing the loch, were blocked up. The former chapel was defined by carefully-shaped round corners.

The Field Club decided to have the chapel walls restored (thatched roof a step too far) and the business of seeking funds fell to Deirdre as secretary. *Awards for All Scotland* made a grant of £5,000 and Jim Ramsay of Corpach began work at Inverbeg in the spring of 2007. A skilled dry-stone dyker, his previous activity included work on walls which featured in the battle of Culloden. Part of Inverbeg was so far deteriorated as to need rebuilding from ground level. Entering into the spirit of the thing, Jim removed stones from the narrow walls of the extension but left a low-level outline of where it had been. Doorways facing each other in the north and south walls suggest welcome to those who walked as well as those who came by boat. During the bracken-clearing a visitor spoke of Inverbeg as the middle of nowhere, but as the artist Ann Dean's display board shows it was once the middle of everywhere.

Large stones for the walls came from the loch side. The floor is paved with small stones different from the pebbles on the beach. There are no foundations. Paul Galbraith says in his book *Blessed Morar*: 'The building itself is of crude dry-stone construction, and was thatched. There is evidence also

INFORMATION PANEL AT INVERBEG

of several dwellings having existed close by the burn flowing down from the hills; and the marks of lazy-bed cultivation on the surrounding flat ground was worked in that vicinity. The priest himself could have tilled some of the land.' Boulton's 1834 estate map (for the new owner Lord Lovat) shows four or five buildings inland from the rectangle of the chapel, with two patches of arable land separated by the promontory's '2 acres 3 rods and 6 perches' of moor providing pasture for a few cows. The priest probably lived in one of these dwellings before he moved, around 1812, nearer to what became the chapel-house and chapel at Bracarina.

This book is mainly about buildings, but people bring life to stones. Not least of these is the priest Ranald MacDonell (1754-1840) whose long mission to Morar began at Inverbeg. Scotland's priests were Mister in the Lowlands and Maighstir in the Gaelic-speaking Highlands until Father came in about the middle of the nineteenth century. *Maighstir Raonull* also appears as Reginald and Ronald. Although his gravestone in the old Morar cemetery has MacDonald, he came from the MacDonell country of Glengarry, and his father probably belonged to one of the MacDonell gentry families: Shian, Drynachan, Greenfield, Ardnabie, Auchteraw, Leek, Aberchalder, Cullachie are all in that part of the Glengarry lands.

Ranald's mother was the second daughter of 'Old Clunes of the '45', otherwise Donald Cameron of Clunes (1683-1753). Clunes House at the east end of Loch Arkaig was burned after the Jacobite defeat at Culloden along with that of Donald Cameron Younger of Lochiel at nearby Achnacarry. The retreating Prince Charles Edward Stuart had a meal at Clunes before making his way into Morar by way of Glen Pean. Later Old Clunes's son Sandy brought news of French ships at Arisaig to the Prince in Cluny MacPherson's hidden 'cage' on Ben Alder. It was the same Sandy Cameron who got him across the swollen Lochy river in 'an old crank boat' that Clunes had managed to hide.

There were overseas connections. Near the end of his life the old priest Ranald MacDonell was assisted by a younger one, Coll MacColl. On 9 February 1838 MacColl wrote to Bishop Andrew Scott at Greenock: 'There are preparations in the neighbouring country to this for Van Dieman's Land [Tasmania]. I hear Mr Cameron Clunis who is to send out his son, i.e., Mr Reginald's nephew, has got a list of 200 persons said to be preparing for that Colony. They have sent Mr Reginald who is in health the usual allowance of £15.' The nephew Allan Cameron of Clunes served in the 79th Regiment of Foot which became the Cameron Highlanders. He had a son Donald who founded the sheep run and town of Clunes in Australia's state of Victoria.

North Morar had been sold by Duncan MacDonell 14th Chief of Glengarry in 1768. The priest at Inverbeg thus became a tenant of General Simon Fraser of Lovat and his successors. A pious gloss on family history is provided in *The Catholic Highlands of Scotland* by the itinerant Benedictine monk (based at Fort Augustus) Odo Blundell: 'His mother was not a Catholic, and was unkind to the boy after her second marriage; but he had the happiness of receiving her into the Church on her death-bed. It is still remembered how at one time there were three ministers in the sick room, but one after the other they went away, and so left the priest alone with his mother, for whose reception into the Church he had so long and so earnestly prayed.'

In penal times, when the Catholic religion was proscribed in Scotland, the education of priests took place in small colleges abroad: Rome, Paris, Douai, or Spain. Ranald's entry to the Scots College which had just been moved from Madrid to Valladolid is well documented. Aged fifteen, he had enough Latin to progress. He must have previously studied in the Glenfinnan seminary because he was one of the party taken out to Spain by its master the Rev. Allan MacDonald. The party reached Valladolid on 23 February 1771 after landing at Santander. All six boys were registered as MacDonalds: Angus, Archibald, Austin, Donald, John and Ranald. The youngest of these was twelve, 'poor Archie' who in June was 'far behind' in his studies. In October he and Donald recovered from a bout of smallpox. That month, when the Bishop of Valladolid administered confirmation to seven Scots students, the rector wrote to his bishop in Scotland that 'Ranald begs to be informed of his age exactly.' Only two of the college's fifteen students knew their dates of birth.

There was also an English College in Valladolid, and the Scots wore the same uniform: black soutane and sash along with a loose gown or *soprana*, closed at the neck but otherwise open down the front with long narrow 'wings'. A three-cornered hat completed the effect. In 1773 the soprana was replaced by a fuller cloak known as the manteo, which formed a circle when laid on the ground. The Scots College rector John Geddes balked at the expense, but his students agreed with the tailor and he yielded.

THE SCOTS COLLEGE, VALLADOLID

In the other Scots colleges students attended university classes, but the rectors of Valladolid's Scots and English colleges agreed that 'our only way is to teach our boys at home; because to send them to the public schools, as they are, would be a mere loss of time which would answer very little end excepting to dissipate their minds and fill their heads with worldly notions. In so far as I know, there is not a master of Latin in Valladolid who knows so much Latin as little Angus MacDonald here.' Little Angus was a son of the Morar chieftain and a priest who had taught at the Glenfinnan seminary. Standards had fallen at Valladolid since the expulsion from Spain of the Jesuits who formerly taught in the San Ambrosio house which the Scots took over.

Some of the stresses experienced by staff and pupils in the early years may have stemmed from too much confinement. Of those who came out with Ranald, Archibald MacDonald left in 1774 and joined the British Army. Donald MacDonald did likewise and was killed in Wellington's assault on Badajoz. Lachlan MacIntosh won some money in the lottery and went to Corunna. After plumbing the depths in the Canary Islands, the prodigal returned and was readmitted. A single-mission priest like Ranald MacDonell, Lachlan MacIntosh was to serve Glengairn on Deeside for sixty-three years: 'He generally wore a Spanish cloak of dark material. It was fastened at the neck by a silver clasp.'

Rector John Geddes was criticised by his first deputy in Spain, and by the bishops at home, for not having a detailed set of rules. A man of great charm who had already had charge of the Scalan seminary in Glenlivet (and was greatly admired by the poet Robert Burns in Edinburgh) Geddes preferred kindness to severity. Custom rather than regulation held the community together until he was prevailed upon to produce eighty-one pages of rules in 1778. By the time Ranald reached the senior classes of philosophy and theology Geddes was reassuring his superiors (to whom he was about to return as a fellow bishop) that the students were 'certainly content and, I venture to say, they have reason to be so: we have got rid of those who gave us any trouble. For almost this twelvemonth past, I do not remember to have heard a disagreeable word in the house.'

Letters home contain detail on life in the house, memories of which would stay with Ranald MacDonell in the very different circumstances of Morar. Among the items imported into Spain was a backgammon table, and the rector was 'petitioned to commission for a Collection of Scots Songs; but if you send them you must see that they be good, or cut out the exceptionable ones' – this from the man who was so much admired by Burns the bawdy bard. Singing was taught

THE CHAPEL IN THE SCOTS COLLEGE

by a Spaniard to masters as well as boys, 'and even *I* hope to be able to sing a Preface, a *Pater Noster* etc.' It becomes possible to imagine the Lord's Prayer being sung in Latin plainchant under the thatch at Inverbeg. Like rural Scots priests everywhere, Ranald MacDonald had to work his own small croft, and spades were ordered for the students at San Ambrosio: 'One is rather insufficient for a dozen of gardeners. A book upon gardening is also wished for.'

A contrast suggests itself between Spain's ornate churches and the humble chapel at Inverbeg. The college one was in the baroque style with a high domed ceiling, plastered and painted with elaborate pillars above the altar. Dreams of Spanish grandeur were further encouraged when he was ordained near Segovia half way between Valladolid and the capital. The ceremony took place in a chapel of the Bourbon Palace at St Ildefonse. College records show 1780 for Ranald's ordination. More precisely the rector's diary has Geddes (and obviously the ordinand) 'at St Ildefonso in the end of July'.

That summer Ranald MacDonell came to Morar. His predecessor James Hugh MacDonald signed himself as 'priest of Morar', having previously served Knoydart, Morar and Arisaig from the north side of Loch Nevis. The chronicler Odo Blundell knew nothing of a chapel at Inverbeg: 'Mr Ronald (Reginald) M'Donell had no house of his own, but according to the custom of the time, stayed one week in one house, a second week in another, and so on, from the end of Loch Nevis to Mallaig.' According to a report of 1783 he had 460 Catholics in North Morar, 250 in South Morar (as far as Glenancross in the Arisaig direction) and 46 at the west end of Loch Arkaig. His North Morar pastoral work took him to settlements on the shore of Loch Nevis from Stoule and Earnsaig to Finiskaig at the head of the loch. There is no way of knowing when Inverbeg began to draw worshippers from all directions, but attention now shifts to later chapels at Tarbert.

2 - Chapel-building at Tarbert

The Gaelic *tairbeart* means an isthmus or narrow stretch of land between two expanses of water, in this case fresh water Loch Morar and salt water Loch Nevis. Tarbert, near the Kyles or narrows between Morar and Knoydart, became a great fishing centre in the nineteenth century. Earlier the focus had been Loch Hourn on the north side of Knoydart. Opening into the Sound of Sleat between Skye and the mainland, it drew in great shoals of herring. According to a Report to the Lords of the Treasury about the possibilities of developing a Highland fishing industry, 'At Loch-Urn, in 1767 or 1768, they came in in such quantity that, from the narrows to the very head it was quite full: such a quantity ran on shore that the beach, for four miles round the head, was covered with them from six to eighteen inches deep.'

The travel writer Thomas Pennant was astonished to find at the head of the same loch 'all the busy appearance of the herring fishery; with multitudes of little occasional hovels and tents on the shore, for the accommodation of the crews, and of the country people who resort here at this season to take and sell herring to the strangers. An unexpected sight, at the distance of thirteen miles from the sea, amidst the wildest scene in nature.' Fishing is a dangerous business, and never more so than when sailing the stormy Hebridean waters in small open boats. Fishermen were superstitious about safety as well as the finding of shoals, and this could extend to religious observance. Shelter for worship was provided on the Knoydart shore of Loch Hourn and then at Tarbert in Loch Nevis, where the herring had 'more of a salmon shape, are stronger, with large black and full eyes.'

Soon after coming to live with the aged Ranald MacDonell, Coll MacColl made Tarbert a particular focus of his pastoral activities. There may have been an older chapel at the head of Loch Nevis. On 25 June 1830 the body of Catherine Gillies was found on the shore at Kylesmorar near Tarbert. Local opinion was sure that her husband Archibald MacLellan had killed her. According to a witness statement taken in the inn at Arisaig village, 'The body was carried to Archibald MacLellan's house and several people watched over it on the Friday and Saturday nights. The body was placed in a coffin on the Sunday morning and taken by the Farm people in a boat to the burial place at Kinloch Nevis.' This was the tidal island of *Eilean Tioram*. No priest was involved, Ranald MacDonell being too old to travel, but three days later the body was disinterred by John MacEachen of Inverie in Knoydart who acted as surgeon for the district. In defiance of all evidence, the verdict delivered at Inverness was Not Proven.

On 11 February 1835 Maighstir Coll wrote to Bishop Andrew Scott, his superior at Greenock: 'The new chapel at Tarbert is very comfortable and I wish we had a heating which we could give it for a triffle.' One of his congregation

TARBERT CHAPEL

was Colonel John Gillies, retired to his family home at Kinlochmorar. The three-storey house which he raised at the head of Loch Morar was accidentally burned to the ground, and the colonel spent his last days at Ardnamurach on Loch Nevis, where his silver military buttons were treasured by kinsfolk. On 26 February 1836 MacColl wrote that he would leave discussion of financial support from Colonel Gillies to the old priest of Morar. Eleven days later he wrote: 'I expect to see Col. Gillies before I return to Bracara,' indicating that Tarbert was served from there.

In the absence of heating he stayed at the inn, as recorded in a letter of 29 March. The tenancy had been reallocated to a new innkeeper and the people were unhappy: 'I am sorry they are a good deal cast down here at Lovat's removing Roderick MacDonell from Tarbert and his brother's widow, both with young families, & when the officer gave the summons he burst into tears with the roar the poor children gave. . . This is no business of mine, but can I shut my ears from complaints altogether? It is a brother of Mr Angus, priest of Arisaig, who has taken the Inn & place of Tarbert.

Undoubtedly Roderick could not keep it so very well, at the same time I found shelter & comfort in it often.'

The priest's last word on Tarbert is curious. On 7 February 1838 he asked his bishop for guidance: 'Wood Cutters and Bark Peelers what am I to do with them unless I exact payment in Confession and give to the owners?' No doubt MacColl would have been told that it was against Canon Law to receive money when granting absolution, although the penitent had a duty of making restitution. There had earlier been concern to protect Knoydart pine trees from fishermen. Nets had to be immersed in tannin and tree bark was the only available source. From summer to autumn at Tarbert there had to be poles for drying and repairing nets and vats of tannin to preserve them. On 22 August 1839 the Rev. William McIntosh, Bishop Scott's vicar general at Arisaig, wrote: 'Mr Coll is busy enlarging his chapel at Tarbert.' Perhaps he was adding 'heating', with accommodation for overnight stays. It was thatched in the traditional way as shown by a letter of 29 November 1882 from the Rev. Donald Walker to Archbishop Eyre in Glasgow:

'The fishing of Loch Nevis has grown into great importance for the last few years and in consequence numbers of Catholic boats come from different parts of Scotland to the loch. At present there is no suitable place of worship at Tarbert. The old thatched place of worship had fallen down before my time and the only place I ever said mass in there was a wool store, which for a certain time of the year was free.' On 15 October of the following year he provided an update: 'Our building at Tarbert is getting on well. I expect the slates today.'

The priest's log gave a full account: 'In Autumn 1882 I began the building of a new slated church at Tarbert, Loch Nevis, which was completed the following summer. Mr

Archibald MacLellan, Mallaig, had the contract for the mason work, and Mr Archibald MacVarish, Arisaig, for the joiner work; both done to my satisfaction.' Archibald MacLellan, whose father Alexander had been a mason in Mallaig for more than thirty years, was soon to be in charge of building St Cumin's at the west end of Loch Morar. 'The people came forward generously and liberally to pay off the debt. Outsiders contributed handsomely. The Most Noble the Marquis of Bute £60. The Right Hon. Lord Lovat £50, and the site. Bishop MacDonald of Argyll and the Isles £30. His Grace Bishop of Glasgow £10. Lord Howard of Glossop £5.'

The Marquess of Bute was a wealthy convert whose generosity to Highland Catholics ranged from the 'Tin Cathedral' at Oban (corrugated iron with a fine interior, replacing a wooden chapel) to a large church dedicated to St Edward on the small island of Canna. Lord Howard, a Catholic younger son of the Duke of Norfolk, owned the Moidart estate. Lady Lovat paid £20 for the interior painting and decoration: no doubt she and her daughter Elsie (who went on to study art in Paris) influenced the design. Visiting from Inverie a year or two later, Knoydart's priest the Rev. John MacElmail reported of the Tarbert chapel:

'The fittings are, so far, of the plainest description, but the walls, lined with wood to suit the climate, have been tastefully decorated by Mr Wilfrid Gettins.' McElmail and Gettins were among the first fifteen pupils at the Benedictine Abbey School at Fort Augustus. Gettins became McElmail's curate at Rothesay on the island of Bute, helping with additional duties for the Marquess at Mount Stuart. Bishop Angus MacDonald of the Borrodale family in Arisaig, who had provided seats and other fittings, came north in September to preside over a service of Benediction.

DONALD 'TARBERT'

Our Lady Star of the Sea (sometimes rendered as Stella Maris) at Tarbert was to have Mass one Sunday in four served by the priest of Morar, with children taught catechism after it. Years before that their parents had attended school in the building. All this high-class patronage was in contrast to the chapel it replaced, but the benefits were soon cut short. When the West Highland Railway reached Mallaig in 1901 Tarbert's importance to the fishing industry ended. The inn closed, its takings reinvested in a new hotel opposite the small station at the end of the loch. The former inn became a post office, latterly run by Donald 'Tarbert' who rowed with mail to the head of the loch. A MacDonald from neighbouring Ardintigh, he recalled earlier times for a book about lost communities, *When I Was Young*:

'When I was young there were plenty of people on Loch Nevis; crofters, fishermen. The tinkers would walk in from Morar to sell their things. There was a market for them. There was a lot of fishing in Loch Nevis. Before the railway, Tarbert was a bigger place than Mallaig. . . This house is a big house. It used to be an inn at the time of the fishing. This was the place where they landed the herring. All the salting and barrelling went on here at Tarbert. . .

'The people here were always Catholics, from way back. The priest would walk over from Morar once a month, or come by pony. The track was better in these days because it was used. Later on the priest came in from Inverie. There was a family down at Stoule – they came up for the services here. And sometimes we would go across to Inverie by boat for services there. On Christmas Eve we'd go to Morar for Midnight Mass. By boat we'd go, we'd be away all night.' Nobody lives at Tarbert now, but Sir Cameron Mackintosh (the *Cats* impresario who bought North Morar from the Lovats) regularly visits the house he built nearby. He has turned the chapel into a bunkhouse for visitors, but it retains a sense of its former use as a place of worship.

*

Having followed Tarbert to the end, we return to Inverbeg. Midway during the half century of services conducted there the priest Ranald MacDonell moved to a more commodious dwelling. A friendship had developed between him and Alexander Chisholm, the richest man in the Rough Bounds. His wealth came from kelp, otherwise tangle or seaweed which was collected, dried and burned so that the soda ash could be used for bleaching and for glass and soap. Chisholm acted as mainland agent for the Clanranald estate, for which the annual income from kelp approached £25,000 during the latter stages of the Napoleonic Wars. In 1811 he moved from a substantial house at Keppoch in Arisaig to the former bishop's seminary at Samalaman in Moidart. At Keppoch he had supervised kelp-making in the workshop of Coll MacDonald (who was also a general merchant) transferring the product to Glasgow by way of Rhu pier on the other side of *Loch nan Cilltean*, the loch of the monastic cells.

This is the background to a letter which Chisholm addressed to the Morar priest from Samalaman on 6 April 1812. The latter's move from Inverbeg had been styled, ironically, as taking up residence in Poverty Hall: 'Your much Esteemed favour of 31st ulto. I only received this day. What in all the world kept you from coming to see me all this time? Depend upon it I shall give you complete dressing the first time we meet – I was informed long ago that you was very busy twixt Arisaig's shops, and the head of Lochmorror, bringing over part of your Furniture & an immense quantity of Crodary ware to furnish Poverty Hall at Bracara – Oh no we must call it, the Hall of Shills and Crowdy & I long to see the inside of it.'

The priest had brought furniture to Kinlochmorar by way of Glendessary from the family home of Clunes at the far end of Loch Arkaig. 'Crodary' may be a reference to crockery: 'ware' suggests it. 'Shills and Crowdy' conveys an impression of modest affluence, shills or shillacks being the lighter part of grain and crowdy a mixture of curd and butter. With an annual supplement of £15 from his relations Ranald MacDonell was more comfortably off than most Highland priests, and he may have also benefited from the kelp 'shops' at Arisaig. Chisholm's letter continues in business-like fashion, making reference to Alasdair Ranaldson MacDonell

15th Chief of Glengarry whose tangle-bearing shores were on the coast of Knoydart. Chisholm's letter ended: 'I do not expect the pleasure of a visit from you till May or till you cut your peats and if you don't come then I shall pronounce you a Rebell!' This refers to family involvement in the last Jacobite rising.

THE PRIEST'S HOUSE, BRACARINA

The building described as Poverty Hall is not much smaller than the combined chapel and house which was later raised on the other side of the burn. As can be seen from inside (though not on the east gable shown in the photo) the original building was a traditional one with walls just above lintel height all round. The corners are squared off, with small stones carefully placed among larger ones and mortar holding all in place. When it was turned into a barn the gables were raised to a point and the whole roofed with corrugated iron. There is a hearth in the west gable, and a walled-up one at the other end less than three feet high. The window in the centre of the rear wall is the same as those to be seen on the front wall - hardly two inches wide on the outside but eighteen inches inside. They look like medieval arrow slits. Perhaps glass was not available then in Morar, but the priest would have had difficulty reading his breviary with so little daylight.

3 - The Chapel at Bracarina

This chapter is remarkable for the detail which has come down to us of building on a difficult site. The first word of a chapel being opened on Loch Morar side comes from a letter written in the clergy-house beside Glasgow's future cathedral by the Clyde. Bishop Andrew Scott wrote on 11 November 1833 to his vicar-general in the Outer Hebrides: 'Old Mr Ranald in North Morar is now unable to do any duty. Mr McColl is at present with him and extremely well liked by the people. The whole of that Mission belongs to Mr Fraser of Lovat, who you know is a Catholic, and has expressed his intention to do something for it in the way of getting a proper chapel. . .' As a boy of thirteen Thomas Fraser had inherited the Lovat estates on both sides of the Highlands, but the title of 14th Lord Lovat had yet to be confirmed. He was the only child of a pious mother and on coming of age he married Charlotte Georgina Stafford-Jerningham. She came from an old recusant family in Norfolk and several of her cousins were nuns. In a letter to the bishop from Beaufort outside Beauly dated 13 December 1834 Fraser linked the end of communal runrig farming with land for the support of a priest:

'I delayed answering your letter respecting the Morar Chapel and lot of ground for the Priest until I saw the surveyor I had sent to lot off and arrange that part of my property. He was detained much longer than I expected having only returned lately. I agree with you that every tenant ought to occupy a distinct lot and that annual changes are most [illegible] to the people. I shall reserve the lot you propose for the Mission & I approve of your plan for the Chapel & house. I have no doubt the people will give their labour in bringing the timber & lime from the sea & collecting the stones which are close at hand & I shall have much pleasure in contributing £100.'

Surveyor Boulton duly produced his Plan of North Morar, lithographed by W. and A. K. Johnston of Edinburgh, in the following year. It shows fifteen lots (later known as crofts) in Bracara. At the eastern end of them is the 'proposed feu' at Bracarina which was to be Church property. (Bracarina is not a Gaelic word, incidentally; it was probably coined by the Lovats.) On the plan no road yet connects the Morar river with Mallaig but a bridle path for leading horses inland from the coast has topped the Bracara brae. Three miles beyond Inverbeg, appears a statement of intent: 'Bridle road to Tarbet lately made in this direction.'

Among other donations for chapel-building was £200 from a Mr H of Preston in Lancashire. In a letter to him of 13 February 1835 Bishop Scott put the Morar project in context: 'This ensuing Spring we must begin to build chapels in six different Missions in the Highlands, viz. Glencoe, Badenoch, Glengarry, Knoydart, Morar and Island of Eigg. In every one of these missions the walls had been built with dry stone, thatched with turf and heath. Part of the walls have fallen down and nearly half of the roofs are blowing away. The people are exposed to wind and rain while they are in the chapel, if a chapel it can be called. There are now neither doors nor windows, and the roof being open, when there is any of wind there is no possibility of getting a candle to burn at the time of Mass but when it is enclosed in a lantern. . . In Badenoch and in North Morar there will be money to build at least the shells of plain chapels, and the rest must stand until more money can be procured.' It may well be that thatched Inverbeg was one of the ruinous chapels described.

The Rev. Coll MacColl had been a son of the manse in Tiree before becoming a student in the Highland District's Lismore seminary and then a priest. He had come to Morar from assisting the aged Bishop Ranald MacDonald at Lismore and Fort William. Because of Bishop MacDonald's blindness Scott felt that MacColl could not have been properly ordained. He feared that the landlord (who was admitted to the Upper House as Lord Lovat in 1837) would be 'disgusted' to find him installed in the chapel-house. In fact the Lovats were to prove very supportive of MacColl in difficult times to come and Lady Lovat presented him with a soutane. By now Scott had made Greenock his base, convenient for the Highlands and Islands in summer. Scott's Glasgow-based deputy or coadjutor, Bishop John Murdoch (also from the North-east Lowlands) took up the challenge of building a different kind of Catholic community.

Scott expected his priests to report fully during a time of challenge for the Highland part of the new Western District. Coll MacColl's letters are packed with information on practical matters as well as human factors to do with his congregation. On 11 February 1835, in reply to a query about the voluntary labour which Lovat assumed would be available, he wrote: 'On Sundays I have been in contact with the Parishioners, and the result is that we find the quarrying and carrying of the stone to the stance pointed at is a work which the people of Morar are inadequate to, considering their unskilfulness in such undertaking tho generally speaking they are willing to do what in their circumstances they can do.

'There is in the first place I may almost say a total want of Implements for such a work & tho I applied for the use of the Roadmakers working Tools I have received for answer that they are not to be had, a later change having taken place with regard to them, that every one of the landed Proprietors of the District must have Implements of that sort for their own Estates. . . In such a case I have proposed to raise a small subscription from £20 to £30 for the purpose which seems to meet with nearly general approbation.' The man on the spot went on to discuss raising some of the money for stone-working from South Morar people who were not Lovat's tenants, and the hope of enlisting 'a Tenant of Glenalladales skillful in these matters'. This man, 'one of our own Parishioners', had visited the site:

'The length of the building he calculated at 80 feet long by 18 feet wide & 12 feet in height with one gable between the House and the Chapel and if the building should be less or more he would add to the £20 or take from it proportionally. I hope therefore that your Lordship will condescend on this much of the Plan without loss of time so that we might get on. It would be better to know the dimensions before concluding a bargain, & if the masons were a month or even less at work the builders might commence and the sooner lime is ordered the better which with the carriage of the slate & timber & sand I have kept for the younger communicants who are unable to furnish money. . . I will propose to the contractor for the stone to make a cart road to the stance which will be but triffling expense.'

A cart road would have been an advance on the bridle path which had been started, but none was made at this time. Nor is there any account of how stones were brought to Bracara. 1835 was a year of slow progress although the builder arrived in the last week of June. Scott's presence in November ensured that lime was finally made available. Winter was no time for building: the walls must have been raised earlier in the same dry-stone manner as at Inverbeg, with mortar added at the final stage. At the height of summer there were three men on the site. Scott learned about the state of interior work in a letter from 'Brackra Chapel' dated 24 January 1836. The writer William Gray had been recruited from the bishop's own part of Banffshire and was married to Scott's sister. His very poor grasp of written English contrasts with the literacy of his son, then at the Blairs seminary outside Aberdeen and destined to become Bishop John Gray in Glasgow.

The letter started with a list of builder's material to hand, mainly surplus timber. Some of it was 'sarking deal' 13 feet by 10 inches for securing slates. Also itemised were nails, including 'scleat nails', and two door locks. The chapel's adjoining house was already glazed, Gray observing that 'there is some weights for windows and a skay light window.' He went on to describe his plaster work on the inner walls (there were to be two layers) and challenging conditions outdoors. He had a local assistant:

'I was up the loch last seterday in purpes to quarry some more flag ther was another boat from this place and angus and me stoped with mr macol's boat until monday as the boat that went with us on seterday was to come back on monday and an other one with his but the wind was very rough they

BRACARINA

could not come angus and me came away from the place about mid day by foot as it became very tempestuous with wind and rain I might have had them all here I depended on mr macoll getting some boats I do not think I will be idel I shurly will get a cam day before I be out.'

When not away seeking flagstone Gray's work was limited by the short hours of daylight: 'I would have been further on if I could have got any candel there was none to be got in arasaig or any other way here about I would rather wrought than ben siting in a dark hous. . . I would not wish that you should get any complaints concerning me neglecting my work. . . I am no ways offended for you warning me I rather thank you for it. . . I was informed the day that the lead was at arasaig.' In another letter Gray commented on the high cost of bringing lead for roofing by cart from Glenfinnan to Arisaig. Timber was brought from Loch Nevis side, but most material was landed at the Rhu pier in Arisaig and transferred to local boats for the coastal stage to the Morar estuary.

After being manhandled past the Falls on Britain's shortest river it was taken to 'the place of boating it to Bracara'. As MacColl pointed out on 26 February 1836, 'What could be looked for but heavy expenditure in so difficult a place as Loch Morar?' Bishop Scott had visited in the previous autumn, staying at Beoraid farm beside the river. As requested by Scott the Morar priest supplied the names of volunteers, most of which are confirmed by the 1841 census:

'These men went from Bracara on a stormy Saturday to meet yourself being at Mr Galbraith's home to unload the Cargo of Lime for the Chapel . . . but the vessel did not get that day to the landing place. . . [They] returned on the Monday following.' Others joined from further afield including Brinacory further up the loch and Cross in South Morar: 'I remember your Lordship was pleased at the exertions they made, it being a heavy and dangerous work they had of it & by which some of them suffered very much in their skins in carrying the Lime.'

MacColl gave Scott an account of subscriptions (six shillings a household) with some postponed until Whitsun. There were also larger donations of £10 from Angus MacDonald of Glenaladale – two of whose sons became bishops in Scotland - and £5 from Galbraith who had the Beoraid farm at the west end of Loch Morar. The sons of crofters were not expected to subscribe but there was work to be done. To anyone familiar with the building at the end of the Bracara road it comes as a surprise to learn that its commanding site was marred by a hillock between chapel and loch. Faith is said to move mountains, but this mound called for manual labour: 'It was not an easy matter, however the people wrought heartily at it, having collected Barrows etc. . . . and also probably more than one half of Cairns of Stones are also removed. . . The stones themselves were made into a sort of Landry Place under the

Chapel.' The *cas chaibe* no doubt came into its own alongside pick and shovel. The laundry was eventually turned into outside toilets for the school which took over the premises in the 1890s. There was no free labour after all but an agreement was reached about 'the number of days' required from each. Those men who moved soil and stone during a busy fortnight were paid a shilling a day, their families' subscriptions reclaimed twice over by hard work.

On 12 March Gray told Scott that the people had got 'the south side leaveled and the east end of the hous it was some difficult to get them to do it right but the place looks very well now.' Following the bishop's instructions in two letters of the previous month the builder had laid gravel round the walls and made a drain outside the upper one. Gray went on: 'I have likewayes pointed the west end of the chapel and portch and chemney neks and squew.' The skew or corner-stone above the west gable would have had biblical connotations for a bishop. A fortnight later Scott told his deputy in the Outer Hebrides: 'We have got a very neat chapel and dwelling house nearly finished in North Morar, the place the most difficult of all others to get materials to.' Much later, between the wars, a croft house was added to the east end of the building.

William Gray's next two challenges were to improve the forty-year-old chapel at Gordon Square in Fort William and to build a new one at Ballachulish for the Glencoe mission. Both were served by the Rev. William Mackenzie who was based in the market town. Gray reported a difficult journey hampered by a sore leg: 'I left north morar on the 22nd march I could not get the tools to arasaig by the salt watter owing to the stormy weather I was oblidged to get them carried over to Cross and got a cart from Mr Dawson to Arasaig.' Cross Farm was a long Scots mile from the Morar bridge. Dawson lived there and had worked as a carpenter on the Bracara chapel along with a MacLean from Arisaig. Coll MacColl found them hard to get hold of as other employment in Fort William beckoned. A metal cross intended to crown the Bracara chapel's west gable was still at Corpach having been landed from a steam boat. Gray left Angus instructions about enlarging the hole if necessary, 'but I am afraid he cannot do it as the foot of the cross is not round.'

The continuing stormy weather forced Gray to spend a night at the Glenfinnan inn, adding to the expenses which he claimed from Scott. In this letter of 5 April he discovers capital letters and punctuation. No doubt help was given by the Fort William priest. Among the various sums listed by Gray was a guinea from the 'Revd Mr Mackenzie advance to joiners'. The £55 which Scott had handed over at Bracara covered several men's wages. Gray also got £10 from Arisaig's priest Angus MacDonald and (in the same district) 'Coll McDonald mertchant account and cash £13 - 5 - 1'. This man's 'shop' was primarily a kelp works but he also provided Gray with goods on tick. Coll MacColl's £17 - 2 completed 'what I have laid out at Morar and what I have received' to a total of £95 - 8 - 1. The builder claimed £22 - 3s for his own pay and expenses which included £3 sent to his wife. She had written asking for support from Bishop Scott in the absence of Bishop Kyle of the Northern District. Gray told Scott from Buckie on 30 April that his wife had received £17 from Kyle during his 42 weeks away, and 'I received from Dr Kyle since I came home £5.'

On 29 March MacColl wrote: 'Neither Mr Reginald or I have determined when to go to the New House & we cannot have Peats for both, & as to the Chapel I fancy it will be heated before we go to it.' On 5 April he explained that one more thing was needful. MacColl had spent the night at Traigh House after going to Arisaig to arrange for 'a vessel to carry home the Seats for the Chapel & timber to finish the altar.' This was a sailing smack owned by Allan MacDonald, who had entertained Bishop Scott under his roof at Morroch near Arisaig village. His letter of 14 April (which ends with a very stylish signature) made reference to his agent. Clearly he was a man of property. MacDonald explained that the vessel had left for Barra with Alex Gillies as master but was daily expected at Greenock. The cargo of prepared timber from Glasgow would be delivered to the bay beside his house at the head of *Loch nan Cilltean* without delay, the vessel being needed for the cattle trade. According to MacColl Galbraith had 'an excellent large row boat just finishing . . . to take it to the Morar River.' The smack was delayed by 'boisterous' weather, however, as the Rev. Angus MacDonald told Scott on 8 May: 'The timber for the Morar chapel at your own request is to be taken out of the vessel without being landed here. Mr McCole is to be over tomorrow morning with two boats to bring the whole & lodge it in the Chappel.'

No record has survived of the opening of the Bracara chapel which, as stated in the Scottish Catholic Directory every year since, did not happen until 1837. MacColl had considered a move to house and chapel in March of the previous year: clearly Bracara became the centre of worship before the formal opening. Perhaps that took place at Whitsun (otherwise the moveable feast of Pentecost) with the bishop in attendance as Coll MacColl had requested. No saint's name was ever associated with Bracara. With the project carried to a successful conclusion the urgent need for letters back and forth came to an end. The next one from Morar filed in Scott's Greenock chapel-house was dated 9 February 1838: 'I have been expecting Mr Stalker over to put up the four seats wanting. . . The delay on Mr Stalker's side may be in some measure attributable to myself being so very often called away this winter, but that does not lessen the reflections of such as are not provided with seats who did not appear for their Interest on the day of letting, but the four if not six new seats will I think silence the most of these complaints to me.' There were as yet no collections taken up in the Catholic Highlands, but seat rents had been introduced to Morar. The Bracara chapel was said to have seated 250, although that is hard to imagine in a space measuring nineteen feet by seventeen.

Finally a letter of 10 July 1838 gives the seal of approval to what William Gray and his builders had achieved in difficult circumstances. Coll MacColl was a popular priest, and his heart would have gone out to the families of Morar in their sodden heather-thatched black houses. However he could not resist expressing to his bishop a satisfaction verging on smug: 'Such weather as we have had since Friday last we have seldom seen the like with continuous rain. . . The whole of the flat part of the country from Arisaig to Lochmorar I may say is one Lake, and today Tuesday the rain continues with very little abatement. . . I am happy however to say that the windows of the Chapel & House resist the rain surprisingly, & that very little water is taken in by them. Few in these countries are occupying a house freer of rain, and I may say smoke if attention be paid to cleaning the chimney.'

Although his bishop had stated that old Mr Ranald was 'unable to do any duty', the register which was begun by Coll MacColl shows him marrying five couples in 1833 at places as far apart as Bourblach by the sea and Romasaig far up Loch Morar. In the following year he officiated at the marriage of Charles MacLean, tacksman of Lettermorar across the loch from Inverbeg whose son was to become a leading flockmaster and politician in Australia. Thereafter MacColl took the main responsibility for weddings in the homes of his people (being 'a great boy for the fiddle' would have ensured him a special welcome) but the Rev. Reginald MacDonell continued to feature in the register.

MacColl's main value to the mission lay in visiting homes now that Mr Reginald was no longer fit for journeys. Travelling with a clerk or altar-server, MacColl brought baptism to children as far away as Loch Quoich and conducted weddings far from Bracara. Vicar general William McIntosh at Arisaig was concerned about one which took place at Swansletter on the edge of his mission. The Moidart priest Ranald Rankin had been supplying and was responsible for banns. On 30 July 1838 McIntosh wrote:

'When I was in Barra, a couple were proclaimed at Arisaig by Mr Rankin the Sunday before I came home, and he refused to marry them till I would return and proclaim them a second time at least; but my good people set off the Tuesday following and got married by Mr Ranald Morar without any line from Mr Rankin that no opposition had been offered. I do not call in question the validity of the marriage, owing to his dotage, yet I have some doubts whether he heard their confessions.'

At a time when whisky was taken by hard-working priests as well as people Coll MacColl ended a letter of 25 May 1838 with a particular request to Bishop Scott: 'I hope you will relieve me from the obligation of keeping spirits constantly in the house on acct. of Mr Rd & lessen the board by £3 instead of it. He can if he likes buy it for himself. He is in the usual health.' As a letter of 10 July shows, MacColl was partly concerned about his own position, every mission priest being supported by an annual 'quota'. In this case it had been channeled through the area's leading Catholic layman: 'Mr McDonald Glenalladale sent me inclosed £19 3s. without mentioning anything about the division of it, & as Mr

CLERGY GRAVES AT MORAR

Reginald and I are near about square at last term of Whitsunday I have left the letter containing the money with Mr R himself until we have the honor of seeing your Lord^{P} or your advice in respect to it. I must be however under the necessity of borrowing a part of it if it belongs all to Mr R after we see yourself which I hope will be soon.'

'Dotage' means mental and physical decay, and in the warm chapel-house which kept out rain the old priest had to be watched. There was no shortage of carers. The first government census of 1841 named three female servants as well as Isabella the daughter of MacColl's nephew in Glasgow. The chimney and the hearth where peat was burned were an advance on fires in the centre of the room, with smoke finding its way out through the roof trees, but there were no fire-guards in Morar. McIntosh passed on bad news to his bishop on 10 November 1840: 'Poor Mr Ranald fell into the fire two days ago and burned his hands severely and cut his face, so that he is in a dangerous way. Mr McColl sent for Dr McCallum this afternoon and I am going to see him tomorrow.' On 29 November the old man was 'recovering though still confined to his bed,' but on Christmas Day 1840 Ranald MacDonald died at the age of eighty-six.

Paul Galbraith: 'His grave is in the corner of *Cille-Chuimein* cemetery in Morar, in the corner nearest to Mallaig. The cross which was erected in his memory became the pattern for such crosses on the graves of other priests buried in the same graveyard.' It takes the form of a low sandstone monument, its cross contained within a circle. This is reminiscent of the Celtic Cross associated with Columba's biographer St Cumin who brought Christianity to Morar from Iona. Like all the other priests whose remains lie here, his gravestone faces those of the people – a Highland Catholic custom looking forward to their confrontation on the Day of Judgement. Meanwhile there have been 'stories among the old people of Morar about miracles worked by him, and angelic lights seen round his grave.'

✠

4 - The Lovats in Morar

In that era of Highland clearances Thomas Fraser 14th Lord Lovat was an unusually benevolent landlord. In the east he made land available for crofters removed by his Chisholm neighbour, and in Morar the population remained steady at about five hundred. After the potato famine which affected the Highlands as well as Ireland Lovat built a pier at Mallaig rather than encouraging emigration to Australia. He was impressed by the West Highland scenery: 'He wanted to have some material for his own use and for all of his keepers to wear. At Morar he was struck with the beauty of masses of primroses and wild hyacinths growing among grey rocks, and decided that the yellow, blue and grey made a perfect combination. So he had rolls of tweed made in these colours. There are no green threads in the genuine Lovat Mixture.' Knitted stockings in Lovat green followed on. The *Breac Garbh* origin of Bracara evokes rough spotted rocks among wild flowers, more picturesque than pockmarks.

Thomas Lord Lovat died in 1875. The new Lady Lovat first entered Morar by dog-cart with her husband Simon in the following summer. She had married him ten years ago as Alice Weld-Blundell and was already the mother of six, but the only other member of the party was her sister Freyda. The cart was left at Beoraid farm: 'There was no road at that time along the side of the loch, but there was a path which we followed and then broke off from it and climbed the hill so as to get a better view. . . It was on this spot that the Lodge was built. There was just sufficient accommodation for ourselves, our six children, governess and servants. As the rooms were very small and we were never there except in summer, we made great use of the verandah; in fact I may say I lived in it, and only went indoors to eat and sleep.' Morar Lodge with its boat house and jetty came into family use in May 1879.

The artistic oldest daughter of Lady Lovat gathered her memories in what became a book as *Avenue of Ancestors*. It was published after her death with an introduction by Compton Mackenzie. Alice Constable Maxwell, as she became on marriage, left an amusing impression of the Lovat family at Sunday worship during their summers in the west. In the east, where the Lovat seating at Eskadale was in an elevated position at the back of the church, the children were permitted to slip out when sermons were in Gaelic and walk home to Beaufort Castle. Not so in Morar:

'The nearest church was at Bracara about three miles further along Loch Morar, and there we used to go by boat for Mass. There was no village, only some scattered houses nearby, but the little church was packed to overflowing on Sundays by all the people who came from miles around. A kind of pew was arranged for us on the gospel side of the altar, so we looked sideways at the body of the church, and for children who were inclined to giggle it was extremely

MORAR LODGE

difficult sometimes to keep a solemn face when something happened which seemed funny. The sermon was always in Gaelic and our padre's continual repetitions of "as you see, my dear Brethren", in that tongue, were carefully counted and sometimes reached the high total of 45.'

By this time the fabric of two adjacent buildings was showing its age, as the priest explained to his bishop on 5 November 1880: 'The whole of the plastering has fallen off the roof of the chapel and house. The chimneys are bad and therefore have spoiled the house. Door and windows are in need of repair. Some slates are wanting on the chapel and house. Cement is required around the chimneys and windows.' On 17 August 1881, following the arrival of the landowner's family, Fr. Walker wrote: 'May I ask your Lordship for the privilege of saying mass at the Lodge for the Lovats? They have requested me to do it for them.' The next step would be to build a more seemly place of worship. On 14 January 1882 he wrote: 'I had Lord Lovat and Mr Peter his factor here last Sunday and the window which was blown in by the first gale was done up for the occasion with all of the old timber I could get about the farm. But His Lordship took no notice of it merely asking when it was done. He said nothing definite about the new building. He complains of having so much to do and I believe it. The castle is going on at home, planting here and a new pier to be erected.'

The Rev. Donald Walker kept a record of progress: 'Lord Lovat, seeing the poverty of his tenants then, was moved to compassion and commenced a new road from the Bridge (Morar Falls) to Mallaig pier, on his own account.' According to the Rev. Donald Mackay at Arisaig, Lovat was thinking of a new church at Beoraid because of the rising number of his tenants in Mallaig. As early as 1842 the previous Lord Lovat, having built a pier to encourage fishing, ordered down to Mallaig sixteen cottar families and provided each of them with a lot. By 1878 there were twenty-three crofter and cotter families in Mallaig and another seven farming nearby.

In 1880 Fr Walker reported that Lovat 'judged it prudent to make seven crofts of the arable land at Beoraid-Mor, for the better accommodation of his people.' There were to be no complaints from Morar when the Napier Commission visited Arisaig to investigate the concerns of crofters. On 22 November 1881 a high tide driven in by a southwesterly gale destroyed boats and houses at Mallaig. Money was sent by Lovat's factor to be distributed by the priest, and new boats and nets were given to those who had lost them. 'The same winter His Lordship sent pigs likewise to the country free of charge to the crofters in order to improve their circumstances.'

But there was to be friction between Simon Fraser 15th Lord Lovat and the Rev. Donald Walker. The priest reported local attitudes on 20 April 1885: 'Lord Lovat still speaks of taking the church down to Beoraid. I told him it would not answer and I have since consulted the people in the matter and they have unanimously agreed that the church should remain at Bracara, to which I fully concur.' Walker's outspokenness on behalf of tenants did not help. Perhaps they had all assumed the new chapel would be on the site of the old one. On 6 December 1886 he wrote: 'The people here never asserted their rights before and the great of the parish take it amiss that they should do it now. All the odium falls on me because I stand by the people.' He was transferred to the Small Isles before the new church rose at Beoraid. When Odo Blundell visited the district in the early years of last century the Bracara building had long since been turned into a school, but Mass was still sometimes said there.

Lady Lovat wrote several books, so it is no surprise to find her young family in unpublished memoirs: 'My fourth daughter was born at Beaufort on the 25th June 1881. The ground was so encumbered with workmen and the noise of chiselling and hammering so continuous that I was glad to get away as soon as I was fit to travel to the peace and quiet of Morar. Little as I knew it at the time, what might have been a terrible disaster took place a few days after the children and I arrived at the Lodge.' The children were Alice (or Elsie) aged about fourteen, Mary eleven, Simon the Master of Lovat nine, Ethel eight, Hugh seven, Alastair five and the baby Margaret.

'The days' doings in the summer at Morar did not vary much; in general they were as follows: the children, governess and nurse started as soon as lessons were over, or earlier if it was holiday time, for the sea. They embarked first of all in a boat on the loch at the foot of the house, and changed into another – a sea boat below the bridge over the River Morar to get to a bathing place. . . On the occasion of which I am speaking the loch was unusually high, the months of June and July having been very wet; consequently the river was in flood. The day's programme had been carried out as usual on the return journey except for a slight delay on the part of the nurse who was in charge. The result of the delay was that Hugh and Alastair got ahead of the nurse and the boatmen, and arriving at the boat on the loch thought they would take advantage of the absence of the authorities to have a row on their own.

'The boat was fastened to its moorings by a reef knot, which is easily untied by those who know the secret of it; unfortunately it was known by the elder of the two, my dear Hugh. The knot being untied they started on their adventure, Hugh of course being in command and Alastair following in his wake, the latter being always ready to follow where Hugh led. All went well for the first fifty or a hundred yards till they got into the current of the stream, and it was at that moment that the elder children and the nurse came in sight and saw what was happening. The boat had just then got into the current and was rapidly approaching the falls; a few moments more and it would have been swept over them and the boys would have come to certain death either by drowning or by being dashed against the rocks at the foot of the falls.

'Fortunately Simon saw at once what ought to be done. He shouted to Hugh to grasp a branch which overhung the stream and hold on to it till help arrived. The men tore round by the bridge, and while one of them got hold of the boat with a boat hook the other managed to scramble into the boat and so rescue the boys.' All credit is due to nine-year-old Simon who in adult life was to found the Lovat Scouts, but something should be said on behalf of the unnamed senior boatman. Neil MacVarish was rewarded for his role in this drama by an additional field at his home beside the post-house in Bracara, and by being given charge of the *Eagle* steam launch on Loch Morar.

Lady Lovat again: 'There was only one chance of salvation which was the overhanging branch, and but for a strong wind which by the Mercy of God helped to drift the boat towards the river bank, the worst might have happened. It was some time before I was told of my sons' narrow escape. Poor Nurse Toomy could not speak of it with any calmness, the agony had been so great, and I forbore to "rub it in" as I felt it was a lesson she would never forget, so there was nothing further to be said.'

*

Having established a residence in Morar, and conscious of his tenants moving westward, Simon Lord Lovat decided that the time had come to provide 'a more suitable place of worship than the former inconvenient and unsightly chapel at Bracara.' The site he chose lay at the foot of *Cruach Bheoraid* looking across to the islands. Then on 6 September 1887, while out shooting with the Mackintosh of Mackintosh, Lovat had a heart attack and died on the hill. His intentions were carried forward with full vigour by the widowed Lady Alice. Father Walker's log for 1888 emphasised local discontent: 'In April the Lord Lovat Memorial Church was begun by Lady Lovat at her own expense. The times were bad and the contractor, Mr Michie, took advantage of the circumstances of the people and paid the labourers at 14/-per week, dearly earned. The most of the stone for the building was taken from the Kinlochmorar Quarries. Boats were paid for carriage at the rate of 5/- and 6/- per day. The people were displeased with this payment.'

OUR LADY AND ST CUMIN'S, MORAR

Paul Galbraith assembled all the available detail, much of it from family sources. Remarkably Muriel the youngest daughter, who was a Sister of Charity aged 104 at the time of the centenary, remembered men wheeling barrow-loads from boats. Grey basalt was rowed down the loch's twelve miles to be dressed on site by the mason Archibald MacLellan of Mallaig. His work included granite facings for doors and windows. MacLellan had overall responsibility for local labour, his own skill extending to the design and completion of the west gable's trefoil window. The space for a statue which he created below it had not been filled when Odo Blundell came to Morar. In later years Archie *Clachair* (the mason) shaped stone for the Kilchumein cemetery's war memorial gate. It was designed by Kenneth Bird the Punch cartoonist and art editor who signed himself Fougasse. Bird married one of the Caldwell sisters at Morar Lodge (long-leased from the Lovats) and their brother John Hay Caldwell was one of those commemorated.

Returning to the new Morar church, we find that a Fraser from the main Lovat estate in Strathglass did most of the joinery. The spectacular roof which from inside resembles an upturned boat was raised by Messrs MacNab. This firm no doubt also slated the tower. It recalls the monastic round towers of Ireland, especially Glendalough, although the church's style of architecture is Early English. All of the 350

THE ALTAR, MORAR CHURCH

sittings were taken for a High Mass to mark the opening and many people were unable to find seats. A full report in *The Tablet* was reproduced in Paul Galbraith's centennial book, having already featured in his booklet *The Morar Cross*. The Gaelic sermon of Bishop Angus MacDonald (who grew up at Borrodale in Arisaig) passed over the heads of lords and ladies in the front pews whose thoughts may have wandered to the prospect of luncheon at Morar Lodge. Along with local people they returned for a second service at six o'clock. As a link with what follows in Chapter 6 it is worth drawing attention to the organ loft where that morning 'the music (Webb's Mass in "G") was very creditably rendered by the choir of the neighbouring parish of Knoydart, led by their pastor the Rev. John MacElmail.'

The local chronicler of all this heard that the first altar 'was an ornate white one that came from the church at Eskadale.' He observed: 'It is interesting to learn that Mr Archibald MacLellan who built the new church was himself married at Eskadale in front of that altar before it was removed to Morar.' In fact Archie *Clachair* was married in Strathglass five years after the church was built. Presumably the ornate white altar came later. It was replaced by another from Fort William when the Gordon Square church gave way to the one beside the hospital in 1934.

Some time after that the Morar baldacchino or canopy was added above with 'O Memoriale Mortis Domini' commemorating the death of the Lord in gold lettering against a red background. Two 'table' altars followed in succession during the 1960s. Facing the congregation to say Mass in English was a revolutionary change following the Second Vatican Council. Canon Ewen MacInnes, who came to Morar in 1968, 'did not hurry it.' The present altar with the Last Supper under it in relief was put in during the incumbency of Fr John Archie MacNeil who died in the sacristy in 1993.

Morar worshippers look towards two stained-glass windows honouring St Columba (*Columcille*) and St Margaret of Scotland. Designed by John Duncan, artist of the Celtic Revival, they replaced two 'richly-coloured' ones put in at the start. Windows in the south wall were donated by local people. One commemorates Canon John MacNeill, the army chaplain who survived his wounds at Paschendaele to serve Morar for many years. In recent times a stained-glass tribute to St Cumin was added to the trefoil window by Martin

JOHN DUNCAN WINDOW, MORAR

Farrelly who also worked on Canna. He learned his skills at Pluscarden Abbey.

We have come all the way from worship in barns and chapels to this church of the high tower. There was to be an even higher symbol. Lady Lovat continued to be mindful of the rescue of her sons Hugh and Alastair and 'longed to put up a monument to commemorate the event and our gratitude for God's mercy. My intention was forestalled by a big cross being put up at the conclusion of a Mission given at Morar a short time afterwards – a good work in which we gladly shared by supplying the materials for it.' Once again Paul Galbraith found an account in *The Tablet* of 3 August 1889. It is

MORAR CROSS

worth noting that the senior Redemptorist priest was Hugh MacDonald, older brother of Angus who grew up at Borrodale. He became Bishop of Aberdeen in the following year:

'Mission at Morar. Sunday July 21st witnessed the close of a very successful mission to North Morar conducted by the Very Rev. H. MacDonald (Provincial) Clapham, and Father Samson, Kinnoull [the Redemptorist house in Perth]. The Mission opened on Sunday 7th July and was held in the new church built by Lady Lovat at Beoraid and opened solemnly shortly after Easter. The services were well attended throughout, not only by members of the congregation but also by persons from the adjoining districts of South Morar and Arisaig. The Bishop was present at the closing services. . . An interesting ceremony then followed, the blessing of a large cross about twenty feet high which had been prepared as a memorial of the Mission. The cross had been fixed up the evening before in readiness for the ceremony on a neighbouring eminence.' The steps are there still, close to the railway line and penitentially steep. A later version of the cross, seventeen feet high and made from iron girders, is now illuminated with lights at Christmas. A view indicator cairn has been added and the steps are improved in concrete with a guard rail.

To continue with *The Tablet*, 'The people, about 600 in numbers, were marshalled for the procession. Colonel MacDonald of Glenaladale led the way bearing the processional cross, and behind him the long line of three abreast wound its way up the hill; the men in front, the women in the rear, joining aloud in the Rosary while children in the centre sang hymns appropriate to the occasion. On reaching the top, the people formed in a circle round the brow of the hill; the cross was solemnly blessed, and Father Samson delivered a stirring discourse explaining the ceremony they had just witnessed. Thereupon the people formed again as before, each one as he passed the cross kneeling down and kissing it, and the procession returned to the church in the same order as it had gone up.'

5 - St Patrick's, Mallaig

Though a good deal less grand than St Cumin's, St Patrick's in Mallaig is also more church than chapel. It was designed by the visionary Catholic architect Reginald Fairlie. His first contact with the West Highlands was when he turned Inverailort House into a castle for the Cameron-Head family by adding a wing. Mass is still celebrated at Inverailort. Fairlie linked church-building with pilgrimage, often walking to sites from his home in Fife - Myres Castle to Fort Augustus for the Abbey church a case in point. His father had been a close associate of the Marquess of Bute and came to Myres from Coodham in Ayrshire when Bute became Guardian of Falkland Palace. Fairlie often slept outdoors, especially at journey's end when he woke at dawn to contemplate what was to become a new place of worship. An associate at 7 Ainslie Place in Edinburgh (Fairlie's residence as well as the firm's office) observed: 'Nothing seemed to be too difficult to him. Churches were born during the night. As a draughtsman he was unique. The way he was able to create a chef d'oeuvre with the minimum of lines was uncanny.'

Of all the many commissions carried out by this remarkable man - they included convents and presbyteries - twenty-eight were new churches. Mallaig's turn came in 1935, shortly after Roybridge and Fort William, with Corpach one of Fairlie's last after the war. Served as it was by the priest at

ST PATRICK'S CHURCH, MALLAIG

Morar, St Patrick's had no need of a presbytery. With a tiny spire and square bell-tower lower than the roof, the building at the top of the main street is strikingly neat with its harled walls painted white. The artist-historian Peter Anson praised Fairlie for his use of concrete and artificial stone: 'To the professional architect the chief interest in Fairlie's churches lies in his willingness to experiment in modern methods of construction and to use new materials.' In this case it was brick rough cast. The east gable of St Patrick's, now stained glass, was originally given three plain windows.

When the church was opened on 15 September the bishop's deputy Provost John McIntosh (a Morar man then in charge of the new church at Roybridge) was the celebrant at High Mass. Canon William MacMaster from Fort William preached an 'appropriate' sermon in Gaelic. The Revs. Dominic and Neill MacKellaig were on the altar as deacon and sub-deacon respectively. A third brother Angus of this Beoraid family in Morar, then a seminarian at St Peter's College Bearsden, was ordained six years later. Father Dominic MacKellaig, eight years a priest at the time of the opening and working in Barra, had prepared for his seminary education in Paris by attending the Abbey School at Fort Augustus. No doubt that connection explains why Gregorian plainchant was supplied by a choir of priests and novices from St Benedict's Abbey. Bishop Donald Martin, who had laid the foundation stone in the previous November, gave Benediction in the afternoon assisted by Canon Alasdair MacDougall and his nephew the Rev. Joseph Gillies. Both of them grew up at Bracara in Morar.

When Oban's 'Tin Cathedral' finally rusted beyond what was suitable for the bishop of a diocese it was replaced by the present building on the northern edge of town. Architect Sir Giles Gilbert Scott also designed Britain's red telephone box. Cathedral windows stored in Oban were claimed for Mallaig by Canon John MacNeill. On the Epistle side of the Sanctuary three Archangels stand side by side: Raphael, Gabriel and Michael. St Michael is certainly appropriate, having been venerated by Gaels down the centuries. Further back, at a level just behind the present table altar on the Gospel side, Zadkiel looks across at Jophiel. Named only in the apocryphal book of Enoch, they are not accepted as archangels in Catholic teaching. The rabbinic writings of Judaism have claimed Zadkiel as the divine messenger who prevented Abraham from sacrificing Isaac, hence his broad knife. Likewise Jophiel has been depicted casting Adam and Eve out of the Garden of Eden. The convert Marquess of Bute was other-worldly, a mystic, and two more heavenly spirits adorn what was created as a Lady altar in the nave of the church. One is Uriel with sacred scroll and book. He is linked, by Anglicans at least, with Confirmation. The other holds a chalice but his name is a mystery of Victorian calligraphy. Names vary in the catalogue of seven archangels who are shared with Islam as well as the Orthodox churches of the east.

Part of this space in the north wall has been claimed for church music, played on the organ over half a century by a grand-daughter of Archie *Clachair*. Archie's father Alexander McLellan had been a stone mason before him, living at No. 18 Mallaig above the East Bay. Helped by sister Anne's son Thomas Wynne, his live-in apprentice, Archie MacLellan enlarged what is now Blair House so as to accommodate four sons and five daughters. Mrs Helen Kennedy, who is still in her father's house, was awarded the Pope's *Bene Merenti* medal for leading the choir at St Patrick's. One hymn with local meaning (and personal meaning for a priest who had been awarded the Military Cross) ends:

Fill earth with blessings of love and of peace,
That all hate may vanish, all warfare may cease;
This world has grown weary of force and of fraud.
Guide Mallaig, St Patrick, and lead it to God!

It was during her time that Canon Ewen MacInnes put it to the congregation that the twelve plain windows in the nave might be replaced by better ones. People subscribed, but – modestly - none of them accepted his offer of having donors named on the new ones.

In 1974 the east gable had stained glass supplied by the Glasgow firm of John Baird, leaders in the field since

ARCHANGEL URIEL IN ST PATRICK'S

Victorian times. Their letter made reference to a sketch by Canon MacInnes: 'The Description of the Design is Purity, Power, Creation and Salvation. Centre Light. The Virgin Mary surrounded by Flowing Cloak to Symbolize Virginity and Purity, the Shadow of the Cross representing Sacrifice surmounted by the Sun and Moon with Sea-Gulls at the Base incorporated with the Sea and Sky giving the sense of Creation and Power.' Underneath she was identified as Our Lady of the Minches, as illustrated by side lights of a fisherman, lamp upheld at the prow, searching for a distressed comrade on a life raft. The four winds are shown at the top. The letter does not say who was responsible for this highly symbolic work: 'The three windows have been designed to

Represent a Creative Element overshadowed by a Heavenly Power.'

Though lacking a gallery, St Patrick's has room for more worshippers than the older loch-side church. The last Scottish Catholic Directory before the Second World War recorded the introduction of a weekday service on Mondays and Fridays in Mallaig as well as 9.30 on Sundays. The motor car brought these two churches closer together. Morar had Sunday Communion at nine (leaving the women of the house free to prepare dinner) and Mass at eleven, with Catechism, Rosary and Benediction later in the day when the women returned. The Altar Society and the Children of Mary were also associated with Morar, although by then more Catholics lived in Mallaig.

Before St Patrick's opened Catholics had gathered for worship in the school, but there was sometimes another possibility. In the summer of 1982 when British forces were active in the Falklands, I 'yomped' (with the march to Port Stanley in mind) into Knoydart along that challenging path beside Loch Hourn – six miles on the map but estimated at twice that on the ground. At Inverie I pitched a tent behind what is now The Old Forge pub, then a kind of club. Inside an old man who was born at the deserted settlement of *Niag-àrd* near Inverguseran told me he remembered Mallaig people coming over to the Sandaig chapel in their boats. Long after this sandy bay and its hinterland lost many people to the last of the Highland clearances, St Antony's Sandaig was 'served occasionally from Inverie.'

6 - Chapels in Knoydart

The civil parish of Glenelg between Glen Shiel and Loch Morar was so large that Established Church ministers based at the Kirkton on its northern edge hardly ever visited Knoydart. Even Protestant Arnisdale on the north shore of Loch Hourn, thirteen miles away from 'Glenelg proper', was too far for a place of worship to be viable. If a minister did cross the water to Knoydart his time would be wasted, as the Rev. Alexander Beith wrote in 1836: 'Though the gospel be preached within the reach of Catholics they will not hear; it is a virtue, in their esteem, so to act.' In contrast to his church, repaired six years previously to provide 'very comfortable accommodation' (to say nothing of a new manse next to it) Knoydart had only 'a chapel, if the half dilapidated and straw-covered hut which serves as a place of worship may be dignified with that name.'

It is possible that this was the 'regular mass-house' at Inverguseran which the General Assembly of the Church of Scotland heard about in 1765. However modern maps show the site of what was once a chapel at Samadalan, on the west coast a mile or so to the south of Inverguseran. *Samh nan Dalaichean*, as the Bartholomew half-inch has it, refers to white billows breaking on flat meadowland. In Knoydart's time of greatest trouble the place was presented to readers of *The Scotsman* and *The Times*, with Glasgow lawyer Donald Ross producing a 30-page booklet on the evictions of 1853. Shortly before this the census officer had found ninety-two people in the neighbourhood of Samadalan.

Eviction was followed by the destruction of their thatched dwellings. Cottar John Mackinnon along with his pregnant wife and six children had their house demolished and furniture strewn about: 'The ruins of an old chapel, however, were near at hand, and parts of the walls were still standing. . . One would think that as Mackinnon took refuge amid the ruins of this most singular place he would be left alone, and that he would not any longer be molested by man. But, alas, that was not to be! The manager of Knoydart and his minions arrived and invaded this helpless family, even within the walls of the sanctuary. They pulled down the sticks and sail he had set up within its ruins – put his wife and children out on the cold shore.'

Much could be said about emigration from Knoydart. It was more or less voluntary in the latter part of the eighteenth century by those who foresaw the threat of sheep-grazing to their pastoral ways with cattle. Then came these brutal evictions by a Glengarry landlord (his mother the driving force) who followed generations of more or less benevolent clan chiefs. Father Coll MacDonald, the first Highland priest to be given that title, organized a relief fund for those of his flock who were forced out: the population of Knoydart was 894 in 1851, mostly in coastal settlements between Inverguseran and Doune. He raised tents in his garden at Sandaig for seven families treated in the same way as the Mackinnons.

When Odo Blundell visited Samadalan at the start of the twentieth century he found the priest's house still standing, although the walls of the chapel had been removed for dykes. That Falklands summer of my visit it was from the chapel-house that I took a stone, although the map said otherwise. My other light-weight symbol to carry home was a hank of wool. The Fort Augustus monk spoke to someone there who remembered when the walls had been high, with 'bracken growing through the doorway, just as if people were coming out of church.'

*

Still on the west coast, the Ordnance Survey one-inch map records another chapel ruin at Sandaig, although it was sound when people came by boat from Mallaig. Blundell's photograph shows an impressive row of chimneys above the two-storey house which was first occupied by the Rev. William MacDonnell in 1849. *The Catholic Highlands of Scotland* described the site: 'Its situation in the Bay of Sandaig, facing due south and beautifully sheltered by the high ground on three sides of it, is most picturesque.'

As ever, the monk took pleasure in human contact: 'At the time of my visit it was tenanted by two old maids who had managed to stay on there in spite of all threats to turn them out. A charming picture was presented by these two old ladies, born as they had been alongside the old chapel-house at Samadlan and now living in the deserted chapel-house at Sandaig.' The 1901 census has Enumeration District 4 beginning at 'Samadalan croft 1 house next Airor Crofters', and then, after a school for the crofters' children and a smaller settlement at Doune, 'Sandick and R.C. Chapel House (occupied by Paupers)'. They were Mary MacDonald, aged fifty-seven and her sister Margaret a year younger – hardly 'old ladies' by today's way of thinking: 'Daily the elder of the two would walk two miles each way to their little croft at Aror. Here they kept a couple of goats the milk of which, though barely half-a-pint, was the greatest dainty in their simple fare. Though there was but one house within two miles of them, the dear old people still clung to the ground they knew so well, and nothing would induce them to move to the village

ST ANTHONY'S, SANDAIG

four miles distant.' The two can be seen with the former chapel behind them. Its cross above the gable recalls the one which was slow to reach Bracara.

More commodious than the chapel at Bracara, St Antony's had seating for three hundred. The warmth of the adjoining house, to which it was linked by a narrow sacristy with a window, would have made it welcoming in winter. The Rev. William MacDonnell was transferred to South Uist within three years of reaching Knoydart and then another young priest, Colin MacPherson, was briefly in residence. It was from Sandaig that Father Coll MacDonald sailed his skiff on errands of mercy, and in its garden beyond the dyke tents were erected. As the Deer Forest Commission was later told, people lived there in tents for three years. When the *Sillery* weighed anchor at Oronsay across the Sound of Sleat, heading for North America with 332 passengers, Coll MacDonald was transferred to Fort William. The Knoydart mission was annexed to North Morar, whose priest was expected to cross Loch Nevis for 'Public Service every fifth Sunday at eleven o'clock.'

One of those who did so was the Rev. Donald Mackay, who wrote to Bishop John Murdoch in Glasgow on 8 November 1858. His letter indicates that the building was thatched before it was slated: 'I duly received your letter informing me of the lead for the Sandaig chapel being forwarded per steamer to Armadale. The last day I officiated at Sandaig I took the lead into my own boat and got it secured at Sandaig. The lead is not put on the ridge yet for want of ladders, Mr Coll having given the one attached to the chapel to Mr McLeod Scottass. I ordered up new ladders to be made at Arisaig. I was out of pocket last year fully £3 for repairs at Sandaig.'

Thirty years later Angus MacDonald Bishop of Argyll and the Isles explained to readers of *The Tablet* that the pastoral challenge of Knoydart went beyond buildings: 'Scarcely a family resides within four miles of Sandaig. Several families live at a distance of of over twenty miles, and there are others beyond these again at a further distance of ten miles. I may mention that one man, living at a distance of fully thirty miles, comes regularly to Mass every third Sunday, taking part of two days to accomplish the journey.' The man must have come to Sandaig from Corriebuidh in Glenquoich, where Bracara's Coll MacColl had baptised the sons of three families half a century before. Slightly less remote,

Kinlochourn was later on record as being served four times a year from Inverie.

*

Since the focus of this book is on buildings, even when ruinous or dismantled, its time-scale is generally limited to recent centuries. However an exception may be made for the *cille* or cell of Kilchoan near Inverie. It was founded by St Comgan, who left Leinster for Scotland in 717 in the company of a monk who gave his name to Strathfillan. Based at Lochalsh, St Comgan was venerated quite generally in the west. Almost half a century after Scotland's Reformation Parliament condemned traditional beliefs, a wooden statue of Coan ('Glengarry's God', as his enemies proclaimed) was burned at the Town Cross of Edinburgh.

One relic of Celtic times is a decorated cross at Kilchoan. In *Knoydart: A History* Denis Rixson has argued that the hole dates it to pre-Christian times, alternatively that practices like betrothal by hand-fasting were associated with it. A round-walled graveyard encloses the cross. Another squared-off one nearby is associated with a distinctly Christian chapel, on the evidence of a kite-shaped stone carved with a cross on both sides. It was either a grave-marker (Bishop Thomas Nicholson learned at the start of the eighteenth century that leading men were buried at Kilchoan) or a boundary cross indicating the extent of sanctuary. A baptismal font has also survived. Just as the Catholics of Lochaber gathered at outdoor Mass-stones, so those of Knoydart would have headed for Kilchoan whenever a priest came to them.

A second Lowland bishop, James Gordon, reached Knoydart in 1707 accompanied by an-interpreter. They had scrambled down the geological moonscape at the head of Loch Hourn to be met by the Glengarry chief's brother,

KILCHOAN CROSS

Archibald MacDonell of Barisdale. His boat took them down the loch, 'there being no road practicable on shore.' After two days resting in what must have served as a Mass-centre at Barisdale they crossed to another gentry house at Scotos. After a month's visitation of the Hebrides the bishop returned by way of Arisaig, and at Scotos he ordained his interpreter as a priest for the West Highlands – the first ordination in Scotland since the Reformation. Hitherto the area had mainly been served by Irish Franciscans and Vincentians who spoke the language. The MacDonells of Scotos provided pious example in years to come and one of them, who returned to Knoydart after ordination at Rome, almost became a bishop. The old priest Angus MacLachlan was living with the family in 1752 when the body of Archibald MacDonell was carried over Mam Barisdale for burial at Kilchoan. Twenty-seven years later the Highland District's Bishop John MacDonald succumbed to a plague in Knoydart and was laid to rest in the same place.

*

There is some uncertainty about where later priests held their services. Vicar general William McIntosh mentioned 'the site of the old chapel' which he was confident the Glengarry family would make available again. This was probably up Loch Nevis at Kylesknoydart, opposite Tarbert in Morar, where the chief's uncle had lived in the previous century. Priests were generally based at Inveriebeg between their two chapels. Little Inverie grew larger as a fishing village and was convenient for journeys on salt water. McIntosh had been a violent whisky smuggler in Aberdeenshire before seeing the error of his ways. Now a campaigning teetotaller, he told Bishop Scott that 'it would not be prudent to collect people so addicted to drink about the Inn there on Sunday.' It was common for drams to be taken after religious services, although Coll MacColl assured his bishop that he had put a stop to selling whisky at Bracarina on Sundays. Inverie had eighty nine residents in 1851 but the adjoining area as far to the west as Scotos only added another eighty. The west coast between Inverguseran and Ridarrach (near Sandaig) had 563 cleared from inland holdings, and McIntosh favoured the establishment of a new Samadalan. Knoydart's priest did not agree.

After years of seminary education at Lismore and Valladolid the Rev. Neil MacDonald had been sent to assist the rector at the Scots College in Rome. Students acknowledged his physical stature as 'Muckle' Neil but did not warm to a professor who regularly came to breakfast with his head in a book. After ten years in Barra he was sent to Knoydart in 1835. McKintosh had been his predecessor in the Outer Hebrides and the two men were in dispute over money owed. As the bishop's mainland vicar general living at Arisaig, his reports on Knoydart's priest displayed a distinct harshness of judgement. Educated at the *grand séminaire* of St Sulpice in Paris, William McIntosh had a high sense of the priestly calling and exerted himself to establish more regular habits among clergy and laity. Prior to the feast of the Assumption in August 1839 he was hearing up to fifty confessions a day at Arisaig while most of his 'brother clergymen' (and no doubt their people) were content with the single Easter communion required by Canon Law. He singled one out: 'I spoke firmly to Mr Niel on the impropriety of not attending better to these indulgences . . . and his answer was that the people would not come to confession.'

This followed McIntosh's first visit to Knoydart. Neil MacDonald's predecessor the Rev. Charles MacDonald had been there for nearly four decades, and McIntosh found that the new man had 'converted the walls of a house which Mr Charles built into a barn, whereas an excellent house might have been made of it; but everything must give way to the idea that the Catholics are to be extirpated root and branch in a few years.' It may be that the barn, for which MacDonald went to collect materials at Arisaig, was intended as a *tigh phìobuill* or people's house as in former days. The priest's belief that overcrowded Knoydart would not keep the graziers at bay for long was accurate (much of the Highlands had already been cleared) so the idea of building again on the west coast did not appeal to him:

'The chapel is wretched beyond description, yet instead of taking the lead and encouraging the people by word and example he actually discourages and prevents their doing any thing, e.g. when he arrived there Mr McDonald Inverguseran had collected £25 to build a new chapel; this sum he (Mr Niel) despised and consequence was that part of the money has either been returned to the contributors or have been ordered by them to be given to Mr Niel for his own private use, and part remains yet to be returned. Now £25 with the people's own labour would build a good thatched chapel.' McIntosh widened his concern to less populous areas up Loch Nevis and the catechising of young people: 'I proposed to Mr Niel to visit them three or four times a year to hear their confessions and look after the youth. He told me flatly that he would not go, for, said he, there were only a few scattered individuals and the youth are quite indifferent about religion. Judge of the man's zeal. How can the youth be otherwise when they are entirely neglected?'

McIntosh now introduced a plan which he was to develop in detail: 'I have thought of another project, till such time as a more zealous and more fit missionary be got for Knoydart, which I now suggest to you but upon which I have not as yet matured my own opinion, that is to annex the north side of the head of Lochnevis to North Morar as they can easily attend at Tarbert on a good day. I will be glad to hear soon from you on this subject. I have more to say on Knoydart but as postage is now cheap I will write to you soon again rather than put you to the bother of reading a cross written letter.' A Uniform Fourpenny Post had been introduced four days before this letter dated 10 December 1839. Uniform Penny Post replaced it on 10 January 1840. Cross-written letters which are indeed difficult to read became a thing of the past.

Details of the vicar general's proposal followed: 'I find that in Knoydart 615 souls are in the vicinity of the Chapel and 328 in the upper part near the site of the old chapel whither Mr Niel never goes to officiate, although you see they are entitled to one Sunday of the three. Not merely that, but taking the half of the population to be adults 117 could attend from Mr Coll's side of Lochnevis and 164 from the three nearest farms of the lower part of the parish [Sallachry, Torrcruin and Carnach] thus making with the half of the population adjoining the Chapel a congregation of 164 + 164 + 117 = 445 adults. So that he might calculate on 300 and upwards every Sunday with ordinary weather that he would celebrate Mass in the Strath or upper part near Glengarry's. And were Mr Niel and Mr Coll to suit their days both sides of Lochnevis might have prayers in their own neighbourhood 2 Sundays of the 3.'

The two priests were on good terms, as shown by a letter from Coll MacColl at a time of unusual cold on the coast: 'I was aware that your Lordship was told of the severe accident which befell me in Knoydart when on a visit to Mr Neil in time of that frost in which I fell and broke my collar bone, which was I believe well enough set by a blacksmith from Skye when the doctor who resides in Sleit did not come to my relief, tho sent for by Mr Neil and myself. In this way I remained with my broken collar bone for the period of six days until that smith came at last and I believe set it well enough, but it gave way two days thereafter and consequently there is a lump on it near the size of a small hen egg; but thank God so much recovered that for the last four Sundays I have been able to officiate, and said the first Mass after the accident at Dallela.'

Dr Coll MacDonald who lived at Dalilea in Moidart decided to let nature work its cure. The bone was not reset, and the Bracara priest was soon able to raise his hand high enough with the host at consecration. Another example of co-operation across Loch Nevis links the more typical rainy weather of the Rough Bounds with reservation of the Blessed Sacrament. The custom of keeping consecrated hosts on church altars - in a ciborium with a lid inside the tabernacle - began in early centuries with the purpose of giving communion to the sick and dying. It developed into a focus for private and public devotion, with hosts renewed every two weeks. New to proper chapels and altar furniture, Highland clergymen like MacColl found themselves with a fresh challenge: 'I have no reason at present to complain of damp in the Tabernacle since I put red hot irons into it. Mr Neil MacDonald of Knoydart suggested this plan & it can be done with little risk with care taking.'

A few weeks later he wrote: 'Where is Mr Neil since he left Fort-William? I suppose still in Glasgow till the meeting of the Friendly Society [clergy finances] be over. There is nothing better for his health than going about for a while provided the Purse be well filled. I was one Sunday since he went away at the Strath of Knoydart, where our own people can easily in any thing of good weather attend as well as the Knoydart people themselves & I intend please God being there also Sunday first.'

In the summer of 1841 Coll MacColl's imminent departure for Australia sent William McIntosh back to the drawing-board. There was a Mass-centre at Inverie, perhaps doubling as a barn, with no restoration of the old chapel at Kylesknoydart. Contrary to what McIntosh had claimed, Neil MacDonald said Mass every second Sunday at Samadalan: 'If Mr Niel would attend once every month at Invereye and

Tarbert alternately, Mr McKay and I could go to Bracara each once every five or six weeks.' The Rev. Donald MacKay was about to begin what he afterwards described as '28 anxious years at Bracara', coming from the Small Isles mission of Eigg and Canna. A month later McIntosh expressed 'some doubt of Mr Niel's coming to officiate at Tarbert either every three weeks or even monthly. However we shall soon see.'

Muckle Neil MacDonald remained another seven years in Knoydart, Samadalan continuing 'miserable beyond description', until his move to the Drimnin mission in Morvern. This made it possible to build the slated chapel and house of St Antony's at Sandaig. Served occasionally from Bracara, the Catholic remnant crept up to two hundred in the 1880s. Following a sharp decline in sheep farming (as elsewhere) Knoydart was turned into a shooting estate by John Baird, a Lanarkshire ironmaster. A team of gardeners worked around his mansion at Kilchoan, family and servants arriving by steam yacht in summer. Baird was well disposed to his Catholic tenants and granted a fine chapel site at Inverie which lay unused for some time. When Fr John MacElmail, educated at Fort Augustus, St Mary's College Oscott, and the Catholic University of Louvain, took over Knoydart as his first mission he lived at Sandaig and walked four miles to say Mass at Inverie:

'Sandaig, the once populous locality in which the church and chapel house stood, had been changed by the cruel evictions into a silent wilderness, and the new pastor quickly realised the necessity of having a church in a more suitable position. But means were absolutely wanting wherewith to carry out the work, until Providence vouchsafed the opportunity through the generosity of Mr Louis de Gonzague Baillairgé, Q.C., Quebec who gave a donation for the erection of a church in honour of St Agatha.' *Ste Agathe* has long been popular with

St Agatha's, Inverie

French Canadians. Baillairgé, a very rich lawyer, rarely left his native city but was in process of founding a church in each of five parts of the world. The last of these, at Sawakin in Sudan, was opened in 1887 according to the Dictionary of Canadian Biography. It contains no mention of Knoydart, although the chapel had opened in September of the previous year.

More from the Scottish Catholic Directory: 'It stands on an eminence looking out upon the broad waters of Loch Nevis, amidst scenery of the grandest description; and it is a pretty little Gothic building, carefully and substantially constructed by Mr Wm. Ritchie, contractor, Beauly. The fittings are, so far, of the plainest description, but the walls, which are lined with wood to suit the climate, have been tastefully decorated by Mr Wilfrid Gettins. For the present, it is only a station, but it is hoped that the day is not far distant when the same kind providence which has provided the Church will also supply the means of erecting a Presbytery.'

We learn from Bishop MacDonald that the cost was estimated at £500. It was built in 1891 when there was still some debt to pay. Father MacElmail moved on to Campbeltown at the other end of the diocese in that year to be replaced by the Rev. George Rigg.

With seating for one hundred and fifty, St Agatha's had a fine choir which sang at the opening of St Cumin's in Morar. Father MacElmail had taken an interest in the new Tarbert chapel across Loch Nevis, and his Fort Augustus schoolmate Wilfrid Gettins provided the woodwork. Gettins, who was to return to the area as Knoydart's priest for a thirteen-year period, no doubt approved the decoration since Lady Lovat's daughter Elsie went on to study art in Paris. She recalled: 'There was another church at Knoydart, not far as the crow flies but it had to be reached via Mallaig three miles away and then by a sea-boat. This chapel had only recently been opened and still lacked paint, so with the priest's approval my mother took her two elder children with her to paint the sanctuary. Having completed that, we thought the two statues would be all the better for some colour. They were certainly more gay when we had finished with them. I hope the congregation thought so too.' When money was being raised for the presbytery one of those prepared to accept subscriptions (along with bishop and priest) was Miss Fraser of Lovat, Beaufort Castle.

Fifteen priests followed Fr MacElmail before St Agatha's closed a hundred years after it opened. Latterly the Sandaig connection brought about a double dedication to St Agatha and St Antony. The future Bishop Colin MacPherson was there as a young priest for nine years from 1942. He gave support to the Seven Men of Knoydart who made a land grab round Inverie. His proposals for breaking up Lord Brocket's 50,000 acres into forty family units became known as the

Father MacPherson Scheme. He should be better known in relation to the Knoydart buy-out of recent times.

Two other priests, both born in Bracara, were there for considerable periods of time. Canon Alasdair MacDougall was in failing health for his final mission during the Thirties, no longer playing – or encouraging – the bagpipes as he had in South Uist. Daily Mass was on offer at St Agatha's and St Antony's, however, and there was an Altar Society which kept religious cloth in good order. Father Iain Gillies began his twelve Knoydart years in 1952. His father Sandy Gillies had been a builder (the croft house added at Bracarina was one of his) with skills which included carpentry. The man who became Canon Gillies at Arisaig had the same aptitude, as Paul Galbraith observed: 'The beautiful ecclesiastical furniture he designed and carved in his workshop now adorns many churches in the diocese. His most notable works in this field included the rebuilding of the church and presbytery at Knoydart which had been destroyed by fire.' He rode from Spean Bridge by motor bike until the house was made habitable. Chapel and house have since been turned into residential property, but Mass is still celebrated occasionally in Lord and Lady Craigmyle's house at Scotos where Bishop Gordon carried out the first ordination in Scotland since the Reformation.

7 - A Cross in South Morar

Divided by Britain's deepest stretch of fresh water, North and South Morar were traditionally distinct. Glengarry's Morar to the north became *Morar mhic Shimmie* when Simon Fraser of the Lovat family purchased it in 1768. The Glengarry connection lingers in the spelling of one of the district's commonest names as MacDonell – emphasis on the last syllable. *Morar mhic Dhughail* was the land of MacDonalds, related to Clanranald but independent of the chief as landholders. The district was described by the nineteenth-century Crofters' M.P. Charles Fraser-Mackintosh: 'South Morar, in its entirety, was a fine property extending from the sea to the head waters of Glen Pean, which flow into Loch Arkaig, and to the sources of the River Finnon, which runs into Loch Shiel. It contained all the waters which run into one side of the historic Loch Morar including also the whole of Loch Beoraid, in itself a grand sheet of water.'

To these topographical points may be added the fact that the flat ground through which the Meoble river flows from

Loch Beoraid used to be known as the Glen of Morar. There is an old burying place on the right bank near its mouth, quite possibly a Mass-centre in former times which worshippers could have reached by boat as at Inverbeg. The crooked Caimbe river which winds its way to the sea through the Moss of Keppoch forms the old boundary with Arisaig. The group of islands at the west end of Loch Morar used to belong to the MacDonalds of Morar, and their oldest chapel of which only a wall remains was at *Eilean Bàn*. This 'white island' was so called because of sandy beaches which are no longer visible due to the level of the loch being raised a couple of feet for hydro-electricity. Bishop Hugh MacDonald, half-brother to Allan Roy MacDonald seventh of Morar, built the chapel along with a substantial house for students. They were moved to a new seminary at Gaoideil, on the north shore of Rhu at Arisaig, and Bishop Hugh also had a house at Bunnacaimbe according to local tradition. Two more chapels are implied. When a Hanoverian force reached Loch Morar after Culloden in June 1746, as noted in the Introduction, it was reported in the *Scots Magazine* that they found the 'Popish Bishop's house and chapel; which the sailors quickly gutted and demolished, merrily adorning themselves with the spoils of the chapel.' A surviving suit of vestments dated 1745 is on display behind glass in the Morar church.

Despite this emphasis on the separateness of North and South Morar in terms of kindred, eighteenth-century priests often had responsibility for both districts. The Rev. William Harrison swore an oath of allegiance before the Sheriff of Argyle at the time of the 'Forty-five and for several years he was permitted to act as priest for the Rough Bounds – all of them. After that, with clergy still in short supply, he took the sacraments to homes in Knoydart, North Morar and South Morar. The Rev. Alexander MacDonald who followed on also

THE MORAR VESTMENTS

served Arisaig and the two Morars. In 1783 Inverbeg's priest had 460 Catholics in North Morar, 250 in South Morar and 46 at Loch Arkaig. By the time William McIntosh was calculating numbers in his role of vicar general the Morar mission, centred on Bracara, took in Meoble, Scamadale, Swansletter and Cross.

There is a clergy tradition about McIntosh exercising his authority over a disputed marriage at the farm of Cross. The bride was from Stoule in North Morar and the groom from Ardnish, otherwise the Braes of Arisaig. He is said to have conducted the ceremony standing at Cross farm with feet in his own mission while the couple remained on the bride's side of a boundary which was largely of his making. For those who enjoy detail and can find their way to the journal of the Scottish Catholic Historical Association, a new level of discipline was introduced for clergy and people (regular Sunday attendance, more frequent confession and communion, local financial support for priests, and marriage in church) in my 'William McIntosh in the West Highlands: changing the practice of religion', *The Innes Review* (Autumn 2003).

ST CUMIN'S WINDOW, MORAR CHURCH

That farm's fuller name is Glenancross, signifying Glen of the Cross. Why? In the seventeenth century many Europeans took up arms for their religious beliefs. The Rough Bounds along with parts of the Western Isles had recently been reclaimed for the old faith by Irish missionaries. In 1626 a remarkable letter (put into Latin by a Franciscan harp-playing bard called *Conchobar Mac an Bhaird* or Cornelius Ward) was sent from South Uist to Pope Urban VIII in Rome.

Iain Muiderteach, or John of Moidart, headed the Clanranald branch of Clan Donald. His letter shows a clear awareness of links with the Celtic monks who came with *Columcille* (St Columba) to Iona and the Scottish mainland. Almost a thousand years before this letter was sent to Rome *Cumine Ailbhe* (Cumine the Fair-haired) seventh abbot of Iona brought Christianity to a wide area from Kilcumein, the old name for Fort Augustus, and Glenelg including Morar.

Seen from another viewpoint, the letter exhibits a zeal akin to that of Islamic Jihad: 'All the Gaelic-speaking Scots and the greater part of the Irish chieftains joined to us by ties of friendship from whom we once received the faith (in which we still glory) from whose stock we first sprang, will begin war each in his own district to the glory of God. . . We take hope, therefore, from the truth and holiness of our blessed religion and faith, to the defence of which we do not hesitate to come, and from the prayers of Your Holiness and of Holy Church whose government you hold. We are confident too, from the fact that these districts are by nature defended and inaccessible and in the power of our nobles and brothers and friends, that it is not necessary to assist us with great expenditure, nor is there desired from your Holiness or from anyone else anything more than a slight assistance, namely four ships well fitted for war and sufficient arms for us to equip 7,000 or so of our subjects.'

This appeal for support took place at an early stage of the Thirty Years War in Germany when Catholics of the southern states were in the ascendant. The 'Catholic Kings' of France and Spain are mentioned in the letter as possible supporters of the Highland project. When something quite similar took place eighteen years later, however, the Earl of Antrim was behind it. Behind him Charles I struggled to control England, Scotland and Ireland as all three kingdoms descended into a state of civil war. In June 1644 Alasdair *Coll Ciotach* MacDonald (Colkitto of Montrose's wars) sailed to the West Highlands with 2,000 men in four ships. By the time Alasdair met the royalist lieutenant general Montrose in Atholl he had been joined by Donald MacRanald, Clanranald's son. The Jesuit Father James MacBreck, who accompanied the army through its year of victories - notably against Clan Campbell at Inverlochy - gives an idea of why a cross might have been raised in Morar. The example comes from elsewhere:

'A brave Catholic lady whose husband was absent, as well as the priest who was her guardian, had her house temporarily invaded by a fresh levy of Highland soldiers passing through the place, for she lived on the lands of a rebel nobleman. She put up the sign of the cross in a conspicuous position in front of her house, declaring it to be a sign of piety not a signal of rebellion, and the commander of the King's forces severely prohibited any insult being offered to the sacred symbol.' This recalls another example at the eastern edge of the Catholic Highlands: 'Calam Griersone, alias M'Grigor, of Baladar, papist, frequently receives popish priests. . . The said Calam [who] was leatly building a chapel for them, erected a very high crucifix on a little hill near to his house to be adored by all the neighbourhood.' The remains of a chapel can be seen in Glengairn near Ballater in Aberdeenshire. By contrast all traces of Alan MacDonald of Morar's mason-built house of 1737 (near an older chapel, it may be surmised) are gone from Glenancross, such was the destruction suffered in the Rough Bounds after Culloden.

The idea of a militantly papist seventeenth-century cross at this farm in South Morar is mere speculation, and a 1610 record of a grant of the lands of Cross argues against it. Denis Rixson, whose *Arisaig and Morar: A History* inclines to calmer possibilities, suggests that a stone high cross might have been

KILDONNAN CROSS, EIGG

erected before the Reformation. His thinking is partly based on the fact that the Morar MacDonald chiefs also held land on the island of Eigg where there is an elaborate Celtic cross at Kildonnan. John Watts, in *Hugh MacDonald: Highlander, Jacobite, Bishop*, raises a doubt as to whether the bishop's father was steadily Catholic. We are left with the evidence of a house having been built by masons eight years before Prince Charles Edward Stuart came to the Rough Bounds and a cross which has also gone from the fertile centre of South Morar.

8 - Kilmory of Arisaig and Clanranald's Cathedral

In her *Wanderings in the Western Highlands and Islands* M. E. M. Donaldson devoted sixteen pages and three illustrations to 'Kilmory of Arisaig'. Till then (her book came out in 1923) it had received little attention. After Kilmory ceased to be a place of worship the roofless chapel north of Arisaig village was known as the *crùisle* or mausoleum, burials having taken place within the walls. The chapel is dedicated to St Maelrubha, an Irish monk of Bangor whose main Scottish foundation was at Applecross. *Loch nan Cealltean*, otherwise the bay of Arisaig, recalls at least one monastic cell thought to have been at what is now the farm of Keppoch. The walls further inland at Kilmory were raised about five hundred years ago. They are three feet thick and ten feet high.

It is often said that Kilmory was one of the six or possibly seven chapels built by a Cameron chief (which one uncertain) after consultation with either Pope Paul III or Gormshuil the Witch of Moy. The consultation was about how to make up for

KILMORY OF ARISAIG

a life of violence. All this is hard to believe, Cameron lands coming no closer than Kinlochiel. Moving to firmer ground, the priest Ruairi Ranaldson was given charge of Arisaig along with Knoydart early in the sixteenth century. According to Denis Rixson he was the bishop-elect of the Isles and brother to John MacDonald of Moidart, the first of the family to be recognised as Captain or chief of Clanranald. Ruairi 'was probably the author of many of the documents connected with the 1545 rising and visited the court of Henry VIII of England. He was literate, cultured, wealthy and well-travelled. Like other important clergymen he was also a patron of the arts.'

This helps to establish Arisaig as the least rough district of the Rough Bounds. Denis Rixson has paid particular attention (words and pictures, one on the cover of *Arisaig and Morar*) to the clergyman who features on a grave slab at Kilmory. It is tempting to see him as Ruairi Ranaldson with the carving commissioned by Clanranald, but a different

CARVED SLAB AT KILMORY

stone marks that man's burial place at Ardchattan Priory. The priest wears the full vestments of alb, dalmatic and chasuble. He is holding a chalice or communion cup. The most curious feature is his headgear, which is different from anything elsewhere and nothing like a bishop's mitre. The priest would have said Mass facing the altar at the east end, his reading of the Latin missal aided by windows on each side wall. The stone has been brought indoors for shelter in the porch of St Mary's Church.

Ninety years ago Mary Ethel Muir Donaldson inspected the mortared walls and detected traces of a slate roof above the narrower 'eke' extension to the west. This small chamber may have provided shelter for the priest. It is notable for a display of the Morar coat of arms (slightly different from those of Clanranald) which is also found at Kildonnan on the island of Eigg. Above, in an alcove facing the entry, is a memorial recording the 'sad fate' of a widow who lost her children one by one after the 1801 death of her husband Simon MacDonald ninth of Morar. His table gravestone takes up much of the space. The only surviving son had an accident at the age of ten and declined from 'fatuousness' to 'idiotcy'. The line of Morar MacDonalds ended with him.

In the opening year of the eighteenth century, Bishop Thomas Nicholson brought the West Highlands and Islands into contact with the Catholics of North-east Scotland, travelling from the castle of his patron the Duke of Gordon at Fochabers. Before setting out for the Hebrides in Clanranald's best boat, Nicholson wrote a report which began with this chapel: 'Kilmaruii, i.e., the Cell or Church of St Malrubber, is close to Keppoch in Arisaig. In this chapel there are several tombs of a hard bluish stone on which there are some ancient figures very well carved, but without inscription for the most part. One would not have thought that the people of these countries had as much skill in sculpture as these tombs show them to have had. There are some on which a priest, wearing the ancient form of chasuble, is engraved.' A priest called Eoin MacMhuirich was presented in 1506 to the charge of Arisaig and Knoydart (no doubt also with the two Morars between) by the combined authority of pope and king so it is perfectly possible that this MacMhuirich is the clergyman whose image has survived. MacMhuirichs were bards to the Lords of the Isles for five hundred years.

*

During the last quarter of the eighteenth century the Rev. Alexander MacDonald of the Kinlochmoidart family was regularly stated in reports to be at Keppoch in Arisaig, and the old mansion house is large enough to have included a Mass-centre. The next two priests John MacDonald and Angus MacDonald (both from Arisaig families) lived at Kinloid a mile or so to the north-east. Angus MacDonald's successor William McIntosh informed his bishop in 1839 that there were 1,213 Catholics in Arisaig and 72 Protestants. Elizabeth MacDonald states in her 2011 booklet *The Church of Scotland in Arisaig* that 'Before the current church buildings were built (for the Catholic population of this district) schooling was undertaken in a thatched house, possibly on the site of what is now the Old Schoolhouse, where Catholic and Protestant children were educated together during the week. On Sundays, the priest and missionary used the school in turn, for worship.' The minister of the extensive Ardnamurchan parish which included Arisaig, the Rev. Angus MacLean, visited in spring from his manse at Kilchoan looking over to Tobermory.

The unnamed missionary was employed by Edinburgh's Society in Scotland for the Propagation of Christian Knowledge. John MacDonald of Borrodale, Clanranald's factor and chief tenant here, had sent two sons to St Cuthbert's College at Ushaw near Durham (a repatriated version of the English Catholic seminary at Douai in Flanders) and one to the Highland District seminary on the island of Lismore. Borrodale was nevertheless content to have his youngest son - who became a priest at Glenfinnan - taught locally in his early years: 'He was most anxious that the S.S.P.C.K. should keep their school in Arisaig and took care of their teacher, taking his side against the local people who liked to engage in argument with him.'

Reginald George MacDonald sixteenth of Clanranald paid for a chapel in the village which was grand enough to be described by locals as 'the Arisaig Cathedral'. It was erected soon after he came of age. According to the 1835 Scottish Catholic Directory, 'upwards of twenty years ago, Mr Macdonald of Clanranald erected a very handsome Chapel for their accommodation in the village of Arisaig; but this Chapel is still in an unfinished state.'

The architect James Gillespie Graham is reported to have designed a 'scheme' for Clanranald in 1813, although a biographer has him at Arisaig three years earlier. By then he was preoccupied with what is now St Mary's Cathedral at the top of Leith Walk in Edinburgh. Gillespie Graham was soon back north for work on Armadale Castle in Skye. Part of the Arisaig scheme concerned the mansion which was raised beside Loch an Eala, but he also provided drawings for a chapel. He was a leading exponent of the Gothic Revival style, influenced by the work of Augustus Pugin whose son and grandson were to be responsible for many churches during the Victorian era.

Arisaig came early. Gothic is most obvious in the double-lancet windows on each side of the porch and the larger triple-lancet one in the east gable at the altar end of the chapel. Above the porch there was a tower, later damaged by lightning and never rebuilt. Originally people entered by doors on each side of the porch in a way which is reminiscent of Inverbeg; the single rounded entrance must have been created after the Catholic chapel became a Protestant kirk. There is no material evidence to show in what way the chapel was unfinished two decades after it had been raised.

Reginald George MacDonald was a pupil of Eton College. After leaving school he became closely involved with rakes led by the Prince Regent. He was condemned for this in

CLANRANALD'S CATHEDRAL

letters by Alexander MacDonald of the Dalilea family at Loch Shiel in Moidart. A shrewd man of the cattle business, he was called the Banker for his financial dealings at Callander. Banker MacDonald wrote: 'Our Chief, I am afraid, is irrecoverable, his disposition is more fitted for the soft retirement of an Asiatic harem than for the rough country to which he belongs;' and again that he was 'very cooly and quietly playing the Devil in London.' Clanranald contrived to gamble away his ancestral lands, selling them one by one to cover debts of £200,000. Hiring Gillespie Graham for the house and chapel project showed that Clanranald had not altogether forgotten his roots (the Highlands were becoming fashionable) but the Catholicism of his ancestors was discarded.

Archibald MacDonald who lived on the point or *rudha* of Arisaig (so Archie Rhu) wrote: 'I hear a rumour through the Country that Clan is to deprive us of the Chaple. . . I am quite distressed at the idea and to crown the Business they say we will not get even the old House. I am very willing to keep possession even by the strong hand until we are otherways accommodated.' Soon after this in the summer of 1825 a visitor's diary confirms that there was a problem. Marshal Alexandre Etienne MacDonald whom Napoleon had made Duke of Tarentum was on the point of crossing from Arisaig to South Uist. His father had helped Flora MacDonald to smuggle Prince Charles Edward Stuart (in woman's clothing) over the sea to Skye. Failing to find provisions in a village with few houses and a 'wretched inn', MacDonald noted 'a Catholic church whose key cannot be found to show it to us'.

With the estate in new ownership after Clanranald the Rev. William McIntosh (now the bishop's vicar general for the mainland) sought to obtain control of the chapel. In the spring of 1839 he wrote to Bishop Scott at Greenock: 'The lawsuit between Lord Cranstoun and Cunningham comes on soon and we must make a desperate push to get the feu when a decision will be made, as I hope it will, in favour of the former.' Cranstoun also owned more valuable acres in East Lothian. He had no hesitation in clearing Rhu Arisaig of its people in favour of sheep, but seemed ready to accommodate the area's Catholics over their place of worship:

'Lord Cranstoun is to give the feu of the chapel, but there is a proposal just now, to which he is inclined to listen in order to get rid of the expences of the parson's house and school house, and that is that we purchase both these houses with an acre of land.' But the proprietor was wavering: 'We have sad work keeping his Lordship on his horse just now. Very serious accusations have been lodged against us collectively and individually so that we are becoming every day more anxious about the feu. We are surrounded by bitter and bigoted and unprincipled enemies. His Lordship has this day refused point blank to give me a lease on Keppoch owing to accusations that I had it too cheap, and this is my return for improving the land at great expense.'

Bishop Scott provided detail in a letter to his other vicar general in South Uist: 'You have probably seen the present chapel at Arisaig, which the Catholics there enjoyed hitherto by sufferance first from Clanranald and then from his successor. It was built solely at Clanranald's expense. On one side of it there was a House built for a protestant missionary in connection with the established Church. A School and School House for the protestant Teacher supported by the General Assembly of the Church of Scotland stood on the other side of the Chapel. Each of these houses are two stories and slated and stand only 16 feet from each side of the Chapel.' Scott assumed that matters were settled: 'We have lately purchased from the present proprietor Lord Cranstoun the Chapel itself, the Minister's House and the School and School House, with a Scotch acre of ground on part of which the Chapel and these Houses stand. It is a purchase for ever, for which we pay for Houses and ground £300 and 7/- yearly of feu duty.'

Despite losing the Keppoch farm McIntosh felt something better had been gained: 'The Minister has a small farm surrounding these Houses, and I have got for the use of the Clergyman a fourteen years lease of the Minister's farm which will maintain at least six cows and a pony. The Minister must remove at Whitesunday first and give up his manse to the priest. To prevent too great an eclat I mean to let the School and Schoolhouse to the present Teacher for a trifling rent on condition that he does not interfere in the slightest degree with the Religious principles of the Catholic children or oblige them to learn anything by heart in the school which the Catholic Clergyman does not approve of. The purchase is making at present some noise among the Bigots and will no doubt irritate the Ministers a good deal. But it renders for ever the Catholic Clergyman at Arisaig independent of any Landlord. He might to be sure deprive him of a small farm but he could never deprive him of his Chapel.'

As events turned out it was a different chapel, as agreed by letters in April 1842 between Cranstoun's legal agent and Sir Charles Gordon the bishops' lawyer in Edinburgh. The Catholic side agreed to give up their rights to the three buildings in the village and were given in exchange an acre of ground near 'the old burying ground' at the nominal feu duty of seven shillings annually. Sir Charles accepted at once without consulting Bishop Scott, drawing attention to Scott's request for three years' further occupancy of Clanranald's chapel while a new one was being financed and built. Reversing the previous decision, Arisaig's priest was given a nineteen-year lease of the house and part of the farm of Keppoch. This was a satisfactory outcome, but about one thing McIntosh was mistaken in telling his bishop that the church in the village was 'only fit to be pulled down.' It serves the Church of Scotland to this day with a pulpit at the west end rather than an altar in the east.

9 - From St Mary's to Inverailort

Odo Blundell typically offered comment on the symbolic return to Kilmory: 'The ancient church and cemetery being both of them full of antiquarian interest and of remains of Catholic ritual and observance, there is a peculiar propriety in the new and handsome house being placed alongside the old one. The two form an example of continuity which is very striking. Justly have the priests in more recent times loved to be buried at Arisaig; there is probably no church in Great Britain which has such Catholic associations. It has ever been surrounded by an almost entirely Catholic population which justly revered, in the time of Bishop Nicholson as well as in the days previous to that and in later times, the ruined church with its ancient tombs and cemetery. In 1700 they had been closed to Catholic ritual and services little more than one hundred years, whilst within the walls of the chapel certainly no other service than the Catholic has ever been held.'

Blundell rejoiced in an age of Catholic triumphalism following centuries of penal laws against the old faith, both in

Scotland and his own Catholic Lancashire. He may have been wrong, however, to say that Kilmory was 'closed to Catholic ritual and services' when Bishop Nicholson admired the quality of its sculpture. Blundell drew upon the obituary of William McIntosh (who died in 1877 after forty years of service to Arisaig and the Catholic Highlands) to describe the transition:

'The Congregation at that time numbered 1,400. There was urgent need of a new church, as the one used by the

ST MARY'S CHURCH, ARISAIG

Catholics was both unfinished and unsuitable in other respects. Mr Mackintosh applied himself vigorously to supply the want. He travelled through part of Great Britain and Ireland in 1845, and with the funds he collected he was enabled to build a large and handsome church, which was solemnly opened by Bishop Murdoch in 1849.' Having come up from Glasgow, the Western District's bishop preached in English and he was followed by the Rev. Donald Forbes of Roybridge in Gaelic. The Scottish Catholic Directory laid emphasis on size: 'In the body of the Church there are no aisles; the whole area of the interior is sixty-five feet in length, by thirty-six feet in width, to which is to be added the chancel, fifteen feet wide by by fifteen and a half feet deep. . . The Church will accommodate from 600 to 700 persons.' Despite the relative size of the two buildings Francis Groome, in describing Arisaig for *The Ordnance Gazetteer of Scotland*, drew a distinction between 'the mission church of the Establishment' and 'a Roman Catholic chapel'.

The Rev. William McIntosh, fresh from his struggle with 'bigots' (not local ones) was determined to make a statement in stone and built high from a low site. The tower of St Mary's dwarfed that of the former chapel in the village. It was only erected thanks to the intervention of Angus MacDonald of Glenaladale who wrote to Bishop Scott on 18 June 1846: 'I merely beg to suggest to your Lordship that you will have the goodness to allow carry thro' the plan as at present fixed on. To do away with the Tower would completely destroy the appearance of the whole Edifice.' Glenaladale went on to point out that the Catholic population was on the rise and attitudes were changing: 'Lord Macdonald's Lady during her residence in Skye last season expressed herself on several occasions very favourable to Catholics – this in itself will be much in our favour and a great check to our Enemies.'

In other words (and despite the rise of the Free Kirk) it was no longer necessary or even desirable for Highland Catholics to keep their heads down. The vicar general planned to add a lead-covered wooden spire with a gilt cross above it. That never happened, but the apex cross finial at the east end of the steep-roofed church was the first of its kind in the Highlands. The clock came later. Another first in the west was the ten hundredweight bell high up in the tower. St

Margaret's chapel in Huntly had led the way with the first legal peals following Catholic Emancipation.

Inside St Mary's the impression of height is still more powerful, with lancet windows above eight-foot wood panelling, an organ gallery in the tower, and - most striking of all - a very tall triplet window behind the altar. At the top was placed an eleven-paned roundel of stained glass by Augustus Welby Pugin, son of the man who influenced James Gillespie Graham. The roundel's crumbling stone was replaced in 2013 at a cost of £20,000, raised during a single year by a combination of local effort and the world wide web.

As well as building high William McIntosh aimed high in the experts that were recruited, his eloquence in pulpits raising sufficient money to pay them. William Burn who designed the church was the son of an Edinburgh architect, his ecclesiastical work in the city including reconstruction of the exterior of St Giles Cathedral for the Church of Scotland and St John's Episcopal Church at the west end of Princes Street. Burn was at the height of his career when McIntosh made contact and had just moved to London. Having provided the technical details of 'lofty interior with timber-boarded ceiling, ribbed and with braces supported by corbels', architectural guide Mary Miers describes St Mary's as 'strikingly austere'. She adds that during the time of William McIntosh the church was 'utterly devoid of ornament', expressing his own stern devotion: 'He was a man of apostolic simplicity of habits, living upon the plainest fare, and spent very little on his own comforts.'

During all his time in Arisaig McIntosh lived at the farmhouse of Keppoch, there being no presbytery linked to the church. A school with teacher's residence above was built beside the road in 1869, and the school later moved to a new site slightly further north. A footbridge over the Caimbe river

THE TRIPLET WINDOW, ST MARY'S, ARISAIG

made it easier for South Morar pupils to attend. The first Ordnance Survey map of 1873 shows that what is now the presbytery or priest's accommodation adjoining the church on its south side had yet to be built. It is likely that Angus MacDonald of the Borrodale family who came to support the Very Reverend Canon McIntosh in 1876 (he died in January of the following year) made this very substantial addition during his short time at Arisaig.

At the restoration of the episcopal hierarchy in March 1878 Fr Angus McDonald became a bishop to Highland Catholics at the age of only thirty-three. Oban was chosen as the cathedral town, but perhaps thought had been given to making St Mary's in Arisaig a true cathedral with accommodation for an episcopal household. Two years later the *Oban Times* reported on a great occasion: 'On Sunday 27th June confirmation was administered by the Right Rev. Angus MacDonald, Bishop of Argyll and the Isles, to 112 members of the congregation of St Mary's Church. His Lordship was cordially welcomed among his former parishioners. He was assisted during the ceremony by the present respected incumbent of St Mary's, the Rev. D. Mackay. The crozier used by the Bishop on this occasion was the elegant one which had been presented to him by the people of Arisaig. Mr Neville of Garramor stood sponsor for the men and Mrs MacDonald, Morar, for the women who were confirmed.' This suggests that Morar men and women (not children as nowadays) swelled the remarkable numbers to fill the pews.

At the start of the twentieth century, when another Angus MacDonald was priest at Arisaig, the interior of the church was renovated and a carved wooden reredos or altar screen was added. Above it in 1906 a striking stained-glass crucifixion scene was put in, designed by Horatio Walpole Lonsdale and made by the firm of W. Gualbert Saunders at Covent Garden. The quality of work produced there was notable for its flesh colour: 'This is unique, had no precedents and has had no imitators.' Comparison may be made with another combined effort by these two men in County Cork: 'The impact created by all these glowing coloured religious images is overwhelming and intoxicating. To enter St Fin Barre's Cathedral is an experience unparalleled in Ireland and rarely matched elsewhere.'

The window was paid for by the Dowager Marchioness of Bute who is shown praying at the foot of the left hand window. Gwendoline FitzAlan-Howard was the oldest daughter of Lord Howard of Glossop, proprietor of the Lochshiel estate in Moidart. From an old English family of Catholic recusants, she married the wealthy convert John Crichton-Stuart third Marquess of Bute in 1872. His gift of a cathedral at Oban has been noted in Chapter 5. In 1890 Lady Bute raised St Edward's at Sanday on the island of Canna in memory of her father. The Arisaig window commemorated her husband after she was widowed. Having followed him to the grave at Mount Stuart on the island of Bute she and their four children took his heart, as requested by the Marquess, to be buried at the spot where Jesus wept over the fate of Jerusalem.

On a more cheerful note, Allan MacDonald has written for the local magazine *West Word* about Canon Iain Gillies (there is a small housing estate named after him) who came from Knoydart in 1968. Allan recalls his English bull terrier, which knew Fr Gillies, keeping him in the house for two hours when he dropped by for a brief pastoral visit. Canon Gillies left his mark – Allan MacDonald: 'When he arrived in Arisaig St Mary's was in urgent need of refurbishment and he set about the task with his usual good cheer, convincing the congregation that it could be done. With fund-raising and planning, he oversaw the whole operation to its completion. He was an excellent carpenter, as was his father before him, and he built church furniture in his workshop.' Not the least of the Canon's work in wood was the creation of table altars for the new 'vernacular' Mass (no longer in Latin) with priests facing the people. The sanctuary below the high triplet window was created by him in the early 1960s. 'Another of his successful projects was to utilise a Job Creation Scheme in the

1970s with which the *Crùisle* (the old church) was prevented from further collapse.'

*

The same Allan MacDonald drew on local tradition to identify the place where the Rev. William McIntosh stabled his horse beside the chapel at Polnish in the Braes of Arisaig. This rugged peninsula appears on maps as Ardnish. The white-painted building beside the railway was opened by Arisaig's priest four years before his death. It was convenient for the settlement of Mullochbuie, less so for the majority of Ardnish people who lived at Sloch, Glasnacardoch, Peanmeanach and Laggan. They had their own journeys to make when the priest rode the nine miles from Arisaig. Clergymen had been serving the Braes at least from the time of McIntosh's predecessor Angus MacDonald. His extra distance setting out from Kinloid is on record: 'About ten miles further up the country there is another Chapel, where public service is performed once in three weeks.' It would have been thatched and as basic as the houses of the people who worshipped there. Mass was said once a month when Odo Blundell came to Polnish:

'Less well known is the little church in the Braes of Arisaig, yet I well remember the Sunday when I visited it. It was a beautiful October morning, and the scenery down Loch Ailort on the one side, and towards Arisaig on the other, was very striking. The congregation soon filled the little church, and of all the Highland churches I have visited – and I have had the pleasure of saying Mass in most of them – the little church in the Braes of Arisaig has for me the pleasantest recollections.'

Part of his pleasure would have come from being a guest of Christian Cameron and her husband David Head whose money from shipping companies (the Union Castle Line in particular) transformed the house of Inverailort into a castle by the addition of two monumental wings. In his study of Christian's photography, *The Cameron Collection*, Iain Thornber writes: 'Inverailort House was refurbished to a standard it had never known before. Dozens of servants and staff were recruited, the driveway was thronged with several new horses and carriages and further afield sheep were being driven from the hillsides to make way for some of the finest deer stalking in the Highlands.' The couple were drawn to the Roman Catholic Church by the Sisters of Mercy at St Catharine's Convent in Edinburgh. As Highland hosts they received monsignors and other clergymen among their many guests in season. Iain Thornber who was often there as a stalking guest of Mrs Cameron-Head recalls hearing the Rev. Sir Hugh Barrett-Lennard singing the Morning Office in his bath. This eccentric priest was on one of his journeys to the Isle of Eigg with boys from a youth group connected to the London Oratory. He became known as the 'Pope of Eigg', and would conduct hunts for an imaginary haggis while making high-pitched shrieks like a peacock.

Blundell's name is also in the Visitors Book. Our Lady of the Braes at Polnish, to which the pious were conducted in the estate's carriages, would have been a pretty sight on the hill above. It is no longer pretty, having been sold by the diocese and never turned into a second home – largely due to planning regulations. Pauline Cameron-Head put in a stained-glass window to honour those buried over many years at *Innis na Cuilce*, the island of reeds in the Ailort river. While the chapel was still in use there was deterioration inside. Mrs Monti Farrell, mother of Mrs Cameron-Head, used to say that it was rather like sitting under a pier with the tide out – such was the vegetation on the inner walls. Mass was last said

OUR LADY OF THE BRAES, POLNISH

there in 1980, and now white paint hangs off the outer walls. This is in sad contrast to what was once a popular picture postcard with a steam train going past.

Ardnish was depopulated before the last war, and then it became a training area for commandos. Inverailort Castle, requisitioned by the War Office like a number of other great houses in the area, was knocked about by the rough soldiery. After the war it was given new life by the second Mrs Cameron-Head and her husband Francis who turned it into an open house with pipers, fiddlers and box-players always welcome. In the same Celtic spirit they inaugurated the Glenfinnan Highland Games.

There were to be three chapels at Inverailort. The first was on the ground floor, entered from the hall and notable for *prie-dieux* suitable for private chapels or oratories. The canopy or *baldacchino* above the altar shares the same aesthetic. It was almost certainly blessed by Bishop Angus MacDonald during a four-day stay at Inverailort in 1891 when he received James Head and his wife Christian into the Church. In 1913 guests at the celebration of the couple's Silver Wedding were shown the 'fine new part of the house and the chapel which is only just finished.' This second chapel was upstairs in Christian Cameron's bedroom before marriage and it continued in use for almost a century. Many a commando climbed the stairs for confession before going off to the perils of war. Eventually the stairs became dangerous and the roof ceased to be weather proof. Prayer was accompanied by the plopping sound of buckets filling, and Stations of the Cross were seen to move as water ran down the walls.

INVERAILORT CHAPEL

It is worth noting that a private mausoleum or vault was opened near Glenshian Lodge to house the remains of James Cameron-Head. His wife Christian (who died in grief soon after the military took over her home) was also laid to rest there. At the west end of Loch Eilt cairns commemorate Christian's father Duncan Cameron and her son Francis

Cameron-Head, for both of whom great processions – first carriages, then cars - came to the spot from Inverailort. The third chapel was opened in a dormitory adjoining the second one. Encouraged by Barbara Mackintosh, Inverailort's custodian since the death of Mrs Pauline Cameron-Head, a hard-working local group created a modern place of worship. Dedicated to St Francis of Assisi and St Antony, and served from Arisaig, it was opened in 2006.

10 - Roshven, Samalaman and Glenuig

West from Inverailort a fine road runs down the loch side for eight miles before reaching the inn and a scattering of houses at Glenuig. The road is 'fine' in the sense of providing a late entry to the district in 1966. It was built to allow cars to pass in both directions at a time when single-track with passing-places took drivers from Lochailort to Arisaig, Morar and Mallaig. Less than half a century has elapsed since goods for Glenuig went from the railway station at Inverailort by boat, and mail was delivered by a postman on horseback along the narrow path. He received a hay allowance from the postal authorities for these daily journeys. To continue with the idea of a place at world's end, the clachan of Smirisary further down the coast, long deserted by its former inhabitants, can only be reached by walking tracks.

Before coming to the chapels of Moidart, a place on the other side of Loch Ailort deserves attention. Early in the eighteenth century Bishop James Gordon made summer visitations from the neighbourhood of Gordon Castle in Lowland Banffshire and, as noted in Chapter 6, ordained his interpreter in Knoydart. Moidart's chronicler the Rev. Charles MacDonald explained that a military presence made it inadvisable for the bishop to come into the district: 'Unwilling, however, to abandon his purpose, measures were concerted by which a large number of the Moidart natives were brought within his reach. The Bishop came as far as the Point of Ardnish, while the people, crossing over the hills and descending to the sea-coast at Roshven, were ferried over the bay to the place where he was ready to receive them, He preached, said mass, and confirmed those among them who had been prepared for that rite. The event is commemorated by *Port-na-h-aifrinne*, i.e. "harbour of the mass", a name still clinging to the locality. This good Bishop repeated the visit several times.'

Midway between Inverailort and Glenuig is the newly restored Roshven House which was raised in Victorian times by Hugh Blackburn, a Glasgow University professor of mathematics. His wife Jemima Blackburn was a highly talented painter of birds and animals, and she also conveyed the scenery and events of Roshven in a delightful way. She and her husband were Episcopalians. There are two windows by her, a Nativity and a Crucifixion, in St Finnan's Church at Kinlochmoidart. The ladies rode 'side saddle in long habits over to church at Kinlochmoidart. . . The ponies put their feet together and slid down the Plate Rock where the Jacobites buried their silver that they had brought to sell for the Prince.'

Later generations of the Blackburn family, however, have included a religious sister and a Catholic priest. In the 1939 Scottish Catholic Directory reference is made to Roshven having a 'Semi-Public Oratory'. The Directory recorded that there was a school with eight pupils, two more than the previous year. This implied that they were Catholic pupils. It was a sub-school to Glenuig Public School which, though non-denominational under the local authority, closed for Church holidays. No doubt the parents of these pupils were among the non-family members who worshipped at Roshven. Authorised ten years before by Bishop Donald Martin, the oratory was on the ground floor furthest to the west and had formerly been Jemima Blackburn's studio.

What her attitude to this change of use might have been is unknown. Her husband had a strong dislike of Catholicism and changed his will in an attempt to ensure that the estate would never pass to anyone of that faith. However the couple's three oldest offspring died without issue and Hugh Blackburn could not prevent Alan the youngest marrying Esther MacLaren of Samalaman House, Glenuig, in 1900. Her father in the legal profession rose to the position of a Lord Justiciary of Scotland. She was a Catholic and Alan Blackburn became one. There is a photograph (quality too poor to reproduce) of the professor sitting – significantly? - outside the Glenuig chapel on the day of the wedding. Later that year the new Mrs Alan Blackburn gave a tea party with dancing at Samalaman for the nineteen boys and fifteen girls who attended Glenuig School beside the chapel. Some of the pupils walked from Roshven, there being no school there at the time.

The couple emigrated to British Columbia in 1907 with their four-year-old son Peter. Although Alan was a Cambridge graduate like his father, he sought to improve his circumstances by farming at Ganges on Salt Spring Island between the west coast of British Columbia and Vancouver Island. The cost of building a house pushed him towards bankruptcy, and he enlisted mid-way through the Great War. He served as a captain in the Rifle Brigade and died in 1925 at the age of sixty. Esther returned to Roshven House with Peter. As the last of the Blackburns in life he inherited Roshven and the

THE ROSHVEN ORATORY

oratory was opened soon after. In due course Peter Blackburn married Pauline Post and the couple had nine children. At the recent funeral of Felicity Blackburn, who lived and taught in Arisaig, one of her sisters recalled their three-mile walk to Sunday Mass at Glenuig.

*

Between the modern Glenuig Inn and and the fine Community Hall a sign identifies 'St Agnes R.C. Church' set back among trees. More follows about that. A mile and a half beyond it on a road which ends before Smirisary stands the imposing set of buildings known as Samalaman House – emphasis on the first syllable. In the last two decades of the eighteenth century there was seminary at Samalaman where up to eight boys learned Latin and habits of piety before continuing their education for priesthood at one of the Scots colleges abroad. There had been several Highland District seminaries since the one at Loch Morar but the first to be dignified with a slate roof was raised by Bishop Alexander MacDonald soon after he moved there in 1783. The previous one at Glenfinnan had been too close to the drovers' inn for peaceful study.

At first the bishop was 'living in a poor reeky house on a puckle straw by the fireside,' but he had two thatched black houses by the end of the year and students were admitted. Samalaman functioned as bishop's house and seminary for twenty years, but money was always short as a letter to the Scots Mission's Roman agent makes clear: 'Since ever I was made Bishop, I always lamented the distress of the Highland District for want of anything of a decent house wherein some of the clergy and I could convene from time to time in order to deliberate about matters regarding the good of religion in these parts; but the low state of my finances prevented my attempting anything of this kind till the beginning of June last, when I began to build on this small farm. By this time the wall is near finished and in a month I believe it will be slated. It is allowed to be very handsome of its size; its dimensions are length about 35 feet; breadth 16 feet; height of the side walls 18 feet. I shall endeavour, God willing, to finish the shell of it without loss of time.' Furnishings were ordered from Glasgow to be conveyed in Andrew MacDonald's sloop.

In his celebrated book on the traditions of Moidart Fr Charles MacDonald described clergy and seminarians worshipping separately from the local people: 'The bishops used to officiate in a thatched house which served as a chapel for the congregation, and which was situated near the shore within a few hundred yards of Samlaman.' Bishop MacDonald died on 9 September 1791 before the sloop arrived. Blundell's annotated drawing distinguishes between

SAMALAMAN

the 'Old Kitchen wing of Bishop's house' and the 'House built by Bishop; he died just when it was finished and only his body was brought there.' He also wrote: 'Before the Bishop built his House, a Seminary was in the Square.' Bishop MacDonald was buried at St Finnan's Isle in Loch Shiel but no inscribed stone marks the spot.

Bishop John Chisholm who followed on recognised that the work had been done as cheaply as possible and sympathised with his predecessor. He found that there had been insufficient allowance made for the wet west coast: 'This house, unfinish'd, takes in water through the walls and if not repair'd will fall, and any houses we have on the small farm want thatch which must be got from other countries.' He meant districts. Chisholm went on to say that he was 'oblig'd for the present to have my boys and my few stirks under the same roof.'

A second clergyman was needed, partly for teaching but also for attending to local Catholics - some of whom came across from Ardnish: 'The Missionary at Moydart never preaches in the point of Moydart whose inhabitants convene on all Sundays and holy days to this place where, of course, we must have prayers and preaching. They come here also from the Braes of Arisaig as a more convenient place than the strath of that country, having it in their power to come in boats, so that the attendance of a congregation will necessarily fall to a teacher here, particularly when I am not at home – hence the necessity of one that talks the Gallic language or could soon learn to speak it.' Teaching in Latin is implied for seminarians, though Gaelic was later used in the schoolroom at Lismore. Shortly before the move from Moidart to Kilcheran on Lismore in 1803 there was a great storm which 'carried away many boats, driven in staves against the rocks. Mine was carried away in the air aloft and never seen since.'

Samalaman passed to Alexander Chisholm, Clanranald's kelp agent who featured in Chapter 3. Others followed, including Alexander Stewart, a pious bachelor who had studied in the successor seminary alongside future priests. After further study in France he became sheep grazier to large flocks at Glenforslan above Glenmoidart. Stewart grew rich on mutton and wool before exchanging these overgrazed pastures for small-scale farming in Glenuig. Census records show that a labourer and a shepherd worked under his direction and there was a dairymaid. The house's leading character was Alexander's mother Christian Stewart, who knew all the stories of local families and lived to a hundred and two. Her finest hour came one night when Samalaman was struck by lightning. The Rev. Charles MacDonald, self-styled Priest of Moidart, passed on a seemingly miraculous account of widespread destruction without injury to any member of the household:

'A loaded gun, suspended close to the shepherd's bed and within a few inches of his head, had its barrel twisted and its muzzle fused by the electric fluid without the charge going off. A large stone built into the wall, and supporting a chimney lintel, was violently detached, flung across the room and, after grazing the face of one of the maids, alighted between her head and the adjoining wall. . . The one person who seemed to retain any presence of mind was his mother, who was then nearly ninety years of age but she was a remarkable woman in every way. While the confusion was at its height she gave orders to the panic-stricken servants with a clearness, promptitude and decision that would have done honour to any general rallying his disordered troops.'

Alexander Stewart checked on everyone's safety before returning to his room to dress with care – only to return without trousers. A host at many social gatherings, 'this worthy laird never hesitated in affirming his belief that a special Providence seemed to guard the bedroom in which he was sleeping, this being the bedroom formerly used by the bishops and, singularly enough, the only one that escaped without injury amid the general wreck.' Droll comment by Fr Charles stemmed excessive piety: 'A small corner cut off in the attics also escaped, but as to the particular kind of genius watching over it he was not so sure. It contained his whiskey and stores of wine. Probably it was benign.' The laird died at Samalaman in 1869 aged sixty-four and was buried at St Finnan's Isle. His grave is marked by a sandstone cross now fallen.

Alexander Stewart left the property to his nephew Alexander MacLean, who added a wing before selling it. Two MacLean daughters became nuns. One of them had a narrow escape: she left her bedroom a day before it was shattered by lightning. This Joan MacLean became Mother Athanasius of the Franciscan Sisters of the Immaculate Conception, her convent close to Glasgow Cross. Three sisters lived on in the house unmarried. On 27 January 1877 the Oban Times

Fr Charles MacDonald

reported a tea and ball given by John MacLean at which 'W. R. M. Macdonald Esq. yr. of Kinloch Moidart led off the dancing with Miss Maclean.' Four years later the census officer found Widow MacLean with her son John, magistrate and proprietor, and daughters Anne and Mary. Anne, though older by eight years, outlived her sister. In 1920 Provost Donald MacIntosh, newly retired from the Moidart mission, told Bishop Martin that 'Miss Maclean of Glenuig is trying to find a priest among her Glasgow acquaintances to spend Christmas with her.' Members of the family were commemorated by stained-glass in the chapel. One window is dedicated to Mary and Anne MacLean and another to Donald MacLean, while the Holy Water stoup commemorates John MacLean who died in 1893 as shown on a gravestone at Roshven. Another very tall stone celebrates the two sisters.

The road up Glenuig continues for two miles before descending to the shore of Loch Moidart. The loch is shallow, and at low tide it is possible to cross dry shod to Eilean Shona. Close to the salt water there was once a hill fort or dun, and boats put in to shore beneath it. This was where, after Samalaman ceased to be the residence of bishops, Glenuig Catholics gathered every third Sunday. The priest Ranald Rankin no doubt came from his house at Dorlin to the old haven by boat when weather allowed. Mr Rankin told Bishop Scott that Portandun Chapel was 'so small that a great part of the congregation are outside be it foul or fair.' A note by Francis Cameron-Head of Inverailort provides an alternative name based on the kyles or narrows between island and shore: 'The ruins of the old Glenuig church are at Caolas.' He adds: 'The present church at Glenuig was built by Mr Hope Scott of Dorlin after a rough sketch made personally for him by Cardinal Newman.' This conflicts with the Scottish Catholic Directory (below). Misled by Robert Ornsby's two-volume biography, Cameron-Head confused Glenuig with Mingarry. James Hope Scott was received into the Roman Catholic Church by his friend John Henry Newman, himself a famous convert, on the same day as the future Cardinal Archbishop Henry Manning. The remains of the Portandun chapel were lost when the new road came through.

*

St Agnes' Glenuig was opened in 1861 as Moidart's first slate-roofed place of worship. Father Charles MacDonald, three years into what was to be his only mission, was eloquent in the Directory: 'This new Chapel stands at the lower end of

Glenuig and commands a fine view over that arm of the sea which separates Arisaig and Moidart. The waters of the loch reach within a few yards of the Chapel. It measures 40 feet by 22 and has a chancel 12 feet by 6. While it has no pretensions to any particular style of architecture, it is a neat substantial building.' Sponsors acknowledged did not include James Hope Scott: 'The site and an acre of ground attached to the Chapel have been kindly granted free by Alex. Stewart Esq. of Glenuig, the proprietor. For this great boon the Catholics of Glenuig are principally indebted to the Right Rev. Dr Murdoch, the Bishop of the District, who has defrayed more than one half of the whole cost. The other chief benefactors were Mr Stewart of Glenuig, the Rev. W. Mackintosh, Arisaig, and the Rev. D. Macdonald, Borrodale, who gave the altar.' Father Donald MacDonald (the youngest son) exchanged his duties as the Borrodale family's domestic chaplain for the new Pugin church at Glenfinnan. The altar no doubt came from Borrodale when the family moved to the mansion which is now the Glenfinnan Hotel.

During the 1880s the landowners at Roshven and Samalaman were urging the new Inverness-shire County Council to build a road from Inverailort. Hugh Blackburn informed the councillors that at Glenuig 'there is a School-board School with more than 50 scholars, and a Chapel seated for 300 at which the attendance is so great that there is (I am informed) frequently a crowd outside unable to gain admission.' At some point a vestry was added in the southern wall. The roof was not properly lined, so that some eighty years later rafters had to be repaired. Work was also done on the bell tower. There was never any accommodation for a priest, although three acres purchased from a Dr Martin by Peter Blackburn of Roshven in 1938 were intended for a presbytery. War prevented that.

Glenuig was served from Mingarry in Moidart for many years although there was no road between the two. Father Charles MacDonald, who is commemorated by a window, only made the journey 'occasionally throughout the year'. Summer and autumn Sunday visits to Eilean Shona for children's catechism were more frequent. His successor gave the impression of a steadier commitment: 'Sittings, about 300. Attended from Lochsheil. Public Service every third Sunday of the month at twelve o'clock. Catechism and Rosary in the evening.' In the twentieth century it began to be described as a Chapel of Ease – one built for worshippers too far from the main church to attend – but there was a distinct lack of ease for clergymen. In 1939, when the congregation was in the sixties, the Rev. Patrick MacDonald came to Glenuig from Mingarry every third weekend to hear confessions on Saturday evening. After spending the night in the school house he said Mass at nine and eleven, catechised children at four and held an evening service of Benediction at five. He then carried on to Roshven for a second night away and said Mass at eight o'clock in the morning. Different visiting priests, mainly Jesuits, came to stay at Roshven for Christmas and Easter. A graveyard which had been used by Glenuig families long before the chapel opened (so perhaps an old Mass-site) lies north-east of Roshven House close to *Eilean na Gualain*.

In 1941 Fr MacDonald was transferred to Daliburgh in South Uist and Fr James Galbraith went from Ardkenneth at the north end of the island to take his place in Moidart. They met at the ferry port: 'Father Pat's last word to me on Lochboisdale Pier was to go to Glenuig just once a month because he had intended going there only monthly last summer. The late Bishop Martin told him that once a month was quite sufficient and that just *one* Mass on a Sunday would do!' Father

ST AGNES CHURCH, GLENUIG

Galbraith told Bishop Grant: 'I had not the physical energy required for serving Glenuig adequately. . . Few priests at the age of 45 are fit for it.' He suffered from rheumatism which, on at least one occasion, prevented him from saying Mass at Mingarry.

During Galbraith's second year in Moidart Fr William Bradley C.S.S.R. came to Glenuig from Canna: a Redemptorist linked to the community at Kinnoull in Perth, he was later to spend four years ministering to the Small Isles of Eigg and Canna. There were difficulties over accommodation close to St Agnes' and he had to make do with an empty house up the glen. This may have been his 'little house, "The Abbey"' which had accommodated seventy pupils before the Arisaig and Moidart School Board provided something better.

In July 1943 as Senior Warden, Air Raids Precaution, Fr Bradley gave gas mask drill at Glenuig School. Later that year he left for St Mun's, Dunoon. Father Galbraith told Bishop Campbell that the Redemptorist was unlikely to return, but he did. He left for parochial work in Wales in 1946. The next year he wrote to Pauline Cameron-Head signing himself Liam Bradley as if to assert their shared Irish roots. She had sought his advice. He responded from the Redemptorists' Hawkestone Hall in Shrewsbury with a six-page typescript on what could be done for Glenuig. It started with the long-postponed road from Lochailort which was eventually built through her pressure as a member of Inverness-shire County Council.

A year further on Fr Bradley was back, invited along with her to lunch at Glenuig when School Meals reached that corner of Scotland. An undated letter from the priest to her husband Francis demonstrates a shared interest in Highland history. Father Bradley mentioned his 'wretched book' (never finished) and shared his notes on the Rev. Alexander MacDonell, first resident priest in Glasgow since the Reformation, first Catholic Army chaplain and bishop of Kingston in Upper Canada. Father Bradley finally left for the Small Isles in 1952. In the following year Fr Joseph Campbell wrote from Mingarry that he had 'not yet organised to the full collections from Glenuig following the departure of Bradley.'

It was during Fr Campbell's time that Wendy Wood noted the survival of an old tradition in her book *Moidart and Morar*. A redoubtable Scottish Nationalist who had a house near Smirisary, she witnessed a local custom at the end of the Easter season: 'I was in Glenuig on the Eve of Pentecost, when every hearth in the glen was to be cold, and the next morning the people were to go at the crack of dawn with lanterns to be lit at the fire ablaze outside the church door. From the lanterns the home fires were to be rekindled. Many of the fires are of peat on a flat hearth, and are smoored at night and reblown the next morning so that they are never out till the same date next year.'

On 17 April 1959 a letter was sent to Bishop Kenneth Grant by David Taylor, husband of the Glenuig teacher, concerning a statue of Our Lady of Lourdes. It had become a 'bone of contention' (to the extent of press cuttings) due to objections raised by Major Richard Clegg. Major Clegg and his wife Jane Croll lived at Samalaman House, her late husband having been the proprietor. A photograph taken three years later shows the statue mounted on a plinth against a rocky background which was probably close to the couple's home. Bishop Stephen McGill had come to Moidart to dedicate the statue. In attendance were two senior priests in

DEDICATION OF THE GLENUIG STATUE

purple and one in humbler black – probably Fr Joseph Campbell who was about to exchange Mingarry for Glenfinnan. Letters to the Moidart priest Jerome Ireland in 1964 indicate that the statue was damaged and sent to Glasgow for repairs after being removed because of road-building.

Father Campbell was twelve years beyond Fr Galbraith's upper limit of forty-five when he walked to St Agnes' Glenuig through a summer storm. After driving what was then the gravelled road to Kinlochmoidart, he completed the journey on foot (by way of the Plate Rock or Iron Age dun) in order to conduct a Glenuig wedding in July 1961. A photo of his arrival appeared in the *Scottish Daily Express* along with a full account of the proceedings: shotgun fired, pipes played after the ceremony, and days and nights of ceilidh in the bride's house. Local historian Jean Lawson of Glenmoidart wrote a leaflet marking 150 years of worship. She put the clergyman's journey in context: 'This is a rare glimpse of one of the last of a long line of walking priests. The opening of the Lochailort to Kinlochmoidart road in 1966, together with the tarring of the connecting road to Acharacle past Mingarry, made a dramatic difference.' Canon Joseph Terry, serving Moidart from Glenfinnan in the 1980s, was able to say Sunday Mass in three places driving round by Glenuig.

✠

11 - Further Into Moidart

Moidart is fortunate to have had two priests taking notes - and printing them. *Moidart; or Among the Clanranalds* by the Rev. Charles MacDonald, Priest of Moidart (his own choice of words), came out in 1889 with financial help and encouragement from Lord Howard of Glossop. He owned the Lochshiel estate and spent part of the year at Dorlin House. With the benefit of a French education which culminated at the elite seminary of St Sulpice in Paris, Fr MacDonald was a fine conversationalist in company. He was also easy with people at all levels of society as indicated by the 208 names enrolled as subscribers to the erecting of his memorial cross on St Finnan's Isle. He died at the age of fifty-nine.

Walter Ireland was born in India in 1914. He took the Benedictine name Jerome on becoming a novice at Fort Augustus Abbey, where he had been a pupil. The monk was ordained and then, after nine years, transferred to the Abbey's prep school at North Berwick. Missing the Highlands, as one might suppose, he left the order to become a secular priest for the Diocese of Argyll and the Isles. After South Uist and Barra, where his acquired Gaelic was put to the test, Fr Ireland came to Moidart by way of short spells at Fort William and Kingussie. For the last twelve years of his life he was based at Mingarry. In our own time John Dye, a leading light of the Moidart Heritage Group, came into the possession of a set of weekly news sheets 'cranked out on an old duplicator between 1968 and 1970.' He turned the historical parts into a booklet entitled *Some Priests of Moidart*. Both of these clergymen wrote about their forebears.

*

Bishop James Gordon found his visits from Lowland Banffshire to 'farr west' physically demanding (goat's milk sustained him) as well as frustrating for lack of Gaelic. A division into Highland and Lowland Districts was Rome's solution in 1727. One candidate for the post of vicar apostolic or Highland bishop was Colin Campbell who belonged to the Lochnell branch of the Argyll family. During the 'Fifteen Jacobite Rising Campbell served as a militia officer on behalf of the Hanoverian government, but he converted to Rome and was ordained at the Scots College Paris. Named pro-vicar for the Highlands, he brought two brothers over to Rome – one of them Alexander Campbell of Ardslignish in Ardnamurchan. Alexander became known as *am papanach mor* or big papist. Poor health and clan rivalry (Hugh MacDonald was appointed bishop) prevented Colin's further advancement. As for chapels, he moved between Moidart and Ardnamurchan. Eighteenth-century Campbell graves within a surrounding wall at *Camus nan Gall* near Kilchoan suggest a Mass-site.

Ardnamurchan, Britain's most westerly land mass, is sometimes regarded as part of the Rough Bounds. The missionary efforts of Austin MacDonald show that it might have become part of the Catholic Highlands of Scotland. In 1790 he crossed from Moidart to meet with Catholics at Gortenfern on the north shore. Mass was being celebrated in the barn of Alexander Cameron when the service was interrupted by Mr William Fraser, 'missionary minister twixt Moidart and Arasaig'. Fraser was supported by the Royal Bounty fund and the General Assembly of the Church of Scotland. Canon Law made no objection to the presence of Protestants at Mass but forbade Catholics to attend 'heretical' acts of worship. Fraser demanded that in exchange for his people - who had accompanied him - hearing the priest, he and his Catholics should stay on for Gospel preaching from 'an antient author'. At the end of Mass Fraser went further, barring exit with the help of three 'coarse fellows'. Maighstir Uisdean urged compromise on his congregation, most of whom 'to the number of ten or twelve' had received communion. Taking the sacrament (after confession) was required during the Easter season which ended at Pentecost:

'So having I thought secured their consciences I stood still and desired my people to hold their peace judging neither God nor the church demanded a squabble of us to vindicate our liberty, particularly so fresh from communion table. I only interrupted him once as he was spinning time and told him we were fasting, and going out he making a great bray said Goe tell your Bishop now what you never had to say to him before – I spoke what I really thought that till then I had less or more of their way, but now I had none at all – to the hearing of the people – as that was the day in which more than ever I perceived the majesty of the Catholic ceremonies.'

The priest was a brother of John MacDonald of Glenaladale who led Moidart and Uist people to a new life in what is now the Canadian province of Prince Edward Island.

Austin entered the Scots College Rome at the age of thirteen and completed his studies ten years later when he reached the canonical age for ordination. He must have also been associated with Rome's Propaganda College because he wrote a report on his mission to the Cardinal Prefect there in 1771. Some of it casts light on the Gortenfern incident:

'It is, as I said in my last letter, a very mountainous district twenty miles long and four broad. Thank God, all the inhabitants are Catholics. There are 500 communicants, without counting the children. We have Mass only on Sundays and feasts, when we assemble in the most convenient places. There, after an explanation of the Gospel, Mass is said. The people go to Confession twice in the year, at Easter and at Christmas. Within the district a minister resides usually, but there is no danger from him as regards my people who hate him from the bottom of their hearts.' Twelve years later he claimed responsibility for 1,450 souls, implying many children, and added (with Ardnamurchan, Glenfinnan and even distant Kintail in mind) that '250 of my people are interspersed among the heretics for a distance of at least thirty miles.'

Since Austinscroft appears on maps near Dalelea (four syllables, from *Dail Eilghe*, field of the second ploughing) it is convenient to call this priest Austin MacDonald. Other versions of his name are Uisdean, Hustian, Austen and Augustinus in the Latin of the Scots College register. Regarding service to his native district (with extended visits to Knoydart which he finally served full time) it was said that 'he had always been a man of great piety and unbounded zeal.' He reported to Propaganda: 'On my arrival here I found this station without house or church, without vestments, books or any of those things which help to forward the service of God. Indeed on account of the people being unaccustomed to subscribe, and on account of their poverty, it has cost me much labour and the greatest economy to rebuild this almost ruined church. . . The altar fittings which I have managed to get are less nice than I would wish but necessity, like a good theologian, solves every difficulty.'

The letter goes on to explain that there were three Mass-centres in Moidart, 'one at each end and one in the centre where the people assemble in turn.' This communication prompted an enquiry by the Cardinal Prefect and details were supplied by Bishop John MacDonald: 'I am informed both by himself and by others that his parishioners greatly assisted him in the work. They gave their services free in carrying the materials for the building, and subscribed about eight guineas amongst themselves. Otherwise he received nothing from any source.

'From the time he came to the Mission he always desired to have a house of his own and frequently told me so, in order to be more free to devote himself to his priestly duties and to his own sanctification which he always had much at heart. To this end he stinted himself as much as possible and eventually saved up £30 sterling. This has all been spent on the building and I fear there may be some debt besides, which would easily happen in the case of a man almost too anxious about religious matters and at the same time little versed in business. He has already completed the chapel but his own house is not yet finished; and I am told it will take another £30 to make it fit for habitation.' The Bishop ended with a plea for 'pecuniary assistance' on behalf of Austin MacDonald. During his Knoydart years he made between three and four hundred converts from Episcopalianism in Glen Elchaig, Kintail, before crossing the Atlantic to join his brother and sister in retirement.

The central chapel was two miles from Austinscroft at Langal, where the road turns west after going round Loch Moidart. Father Ireland dated it to the end of Austin MacDonald's time: 'The Langal chapel was certainly complete in July 1778, and was built on the site of an older chapel. Being originally constructed of loose stone and thatch it probably experienced several "re-buildings" in its time.' Another occurred in 1834, on the evidence of Ranald Rankin who was then Moidart's priest. Earlier the Rev. Norman MacDonald, a Moidart man who served his native district for forty years, had written to the Gaelic Schools Society in Edinburgh in 1813 offering Langal as the only building big enough for a school.

In our own time Sandy MacDonald, who worked as a joiner on the Dorlin estate, confirmed a 'house of meeting at Langal'. From Maighstir Uisdean's account of rebuilding an almost ruined church there was obviously stonework and fallen stones: the material carried by parishioners would have been wood for roof and doorway as well as thatch. There is now a private dwelling called The Old Poors House on the site, the name reflecting a change of use. Tim Roberton of the Moidart Heritage Group questioned the owner about the history of her home. Before the four-roomed accommodation for paupers was modernised more than forty years ago local workers dismantled the ruined chapel at the rear. The stones now support a raised flower bed.

*

The third chapel (after Portandun and Langal) was beside Castle Tioram at Dorlin where the Shiel river enters the sea. The castle which is on a tidal island has been a ruin for three hundred years. On 2 July 1825 an interesting visitor appeared, Napoleon's marshal whom the Emperor had made Duke of

Tarentum. Having spent the previous night at the castle of Armadale in Skye, the French MacDonald came ashore at Moidart: 'At the castle's foot, on the east side, lies the Catholic church. It is a miserable hut, isolated, covered with thatch like the others, and somewhat improved. We did not feel tempted to see the inside.'

This slightly improved building may have been as old as the castle itself. A better chapel was raised at nearby Dorlin in the following year. Archibald MacDonald of Rhu has been mentioned in connection with Clanranald's Arisaig chapel which was locked when the Frenchman reached the coast. It was he, as owner of the Lochshiel estate, who made croft land available to the Church, although Moidart's first slated chapel was paid for by Allan MacDonald and his sister Isabella. There was also accommodation, part of which was occupied by Miss Bell. The old priest Norman MacDonald, *Maighstir Tormod,* moved from neighbouring Scardoish to the greater comfort of Dorlin. Two of his cows had died at Scardoish and he was hoping for extra grazing at Dorlin even before he went to live there.

Details appear in a letter by Vicar General William McIntosh to Bishop Scott dated 18 February 1838. The priest Alexander MacDonald, who had come to assist the old man and then succeeded him, was about to move on. One detail about this priest touches on travel around Moidart and also the drink problem which caused his suspension: 'When Mr Alexr was in his glory and half seas over and called to visit the sick, he refused the service of men to row the boat but he must have women, likely young lasses, to ferry him.' As a young teacher at Glenuig Mary MacDonell (who married the Morar chronicler Paul Galbraith) found rowing Fr James Galbraith to be one of her duties. Perhaps this became a Moidart custom. Alexander MacDonald went from the Western District to the

Northern District, only to be suspended for the same offence – a breakdown when visiting the west coast at Kintail. He conquered his addiction in Nova Scotia and became the bishop's right-hand man as vicar general.

Arisaig's vicar general again: 'The house must be rented from Miss Isabella McDonald to whom it belongs as Mr Alexr has never been able to redeem his share of it. There are accommodations enough for both families if they would agree. There are, besides an outer kitchen, a room and bed closet adjoining on the ground floor, and also a garret with a bed or more occupied by Mr Alexr.' The owner and her brother Allan were thinking about going to Australia for his health's sake, but Mr McIntosh considered that continuing the lease was the best option: 'I would not advise the incumbent to purchase Miss Bell's house as in course of time, when people's views are more enlarged, one centrical chapel might be approved of, and then the house would be a clog instead of a benefit where it now stands.' The 1841 census shows Allan MacDonald and his older sister in residence at Dorlin, which also accommodated another five people. Ten years later Isabella and her brother, now a flesher or butcher, were at 26 High Street, Fort William. Her death certificate dated 20 September 1858 shows her to have died from asthma at seventy-two, the daughter of Donald MacDonald of Lochans in Glenmoidart.

The priest who succeeded Alexander MacDonald was Ranald Rankin, and his entry in the 1852 Scottish Catholic Directory provides information on Dorlin: 'There are two Chapels in Moidart. The one at which the clergyman resides is a plain slated building forty feet long by twenty wide, and by far too small for the congregation. It was erected in 1826 by Mr Archibald MacDonald of Rhue, father of the present proprietor of the Lochshiel estate. The congregation contrib-

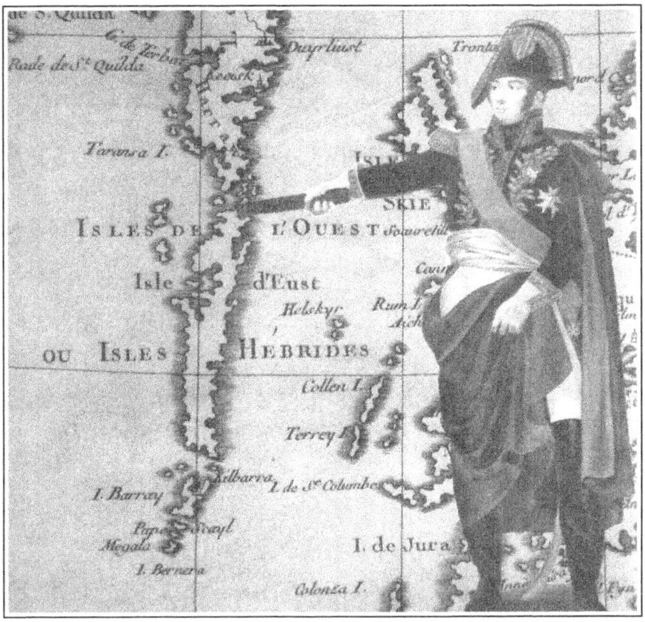

Marshal Alexandre MacDonald

uted a small share of the expenses. Being in an unfinished state, it did not receive the name of any Patron saint; but, from its situation near Castle Tirrim, it is designated the Castle Chapel.' The 1851 census shows Mr Rankin at Dorlin with his sister Jean as housekeeper. An even more crowded house registers another eight occupants. Before moving on from this corner of Moidart, it should be noted that when Dorlin House was built across the river by James Hope Scott in the 1860s it included (on the evidence of local historian Iain Thornber) 'a private chapel and sacristy'.

*

Mr Ranald Rankin did not obtain access to the accommodation at Dorlin until some time in the 1840s. Father Ireland 'heard it said' that he made his base (including a small chapel) at Egnaig beside the North Channel into Loch

Moidart. At the time of the 1841 census Rankin was at Maighstir Tormod's Scardoish sharing the house with another seven. Two years before this Bishop Scott at Greenock had received a letter from his vicar general: 'A centrical chapel besides being in the centre of the country would require to be in an elegant exposure suitable to the building to be erected. Mr Rankin went sneakingly about the business and never asked my opinion. He is tired of attending the three chapels and he wanted the thing done in a jiffy. . . However with a little caution and prudence and patience I do not despair of getting matters to rights again. I will take a step over after Christmas.'

Caution, prudence and patience availed nothing; matters were not got to rights. The Highland potato blight of the late 1840s produced famine conditions which were made worse by the arrival of families cleared from the Rhu of Arisaig. Assisted emigration to Australia followed in stages, the last of which saw the Rev. Ranald Rankin going out to join his Moidart people in 1855. That was the year when James Hope Scott purchased the Lochiel estate. This priest was a poet in the Gaelic language, and he left behind the Christmas hymn *Taladh Chriosta* (The Saviour's Lullaby) which is still sung in the Hebrides.

After visiting the west coast and making the Glenuig chapel possible, Bishop John Murdoch wrote: 'I am in expectation that in the course of this year one of the few Catholic proprietors, a convert to our Holy Faith, will replace a wretched old chapel by a good Church in the heart of his property. He has already provided a commodious school for the children of his Catholic tenantry. He also means to attach to the Church a dwelling house for the priest, who at present is obliged to lodge where he can with one of the tenants.' As the 1861 census showed, Fr Charles MacDonald's new house had fourteen rooms with windows.

JAMES HOPE SCOTT

Some ten years after his conversion to Rome James Hope Scott purchased the Lochshiel estate unseen after a Catholic lady had voiced her concern about it falling into the hands of a Protestant landowner. A wealthy barrister in London, he already held Scottish property at Abbotsford through his first wife who was Sir Walter Scott's grand-daughter. In addition to the church and school buildings mentioned by Bishop Murdoch he built the four-storey Dorlin House in Scots Baronial style. An improved road and a bridge over the river enabled the genteel incomers to be transported by horse and carriage. A close relationship between church and school was established, and later photographs show the Corpus Christi procession from one to the other. Men sheltered the priest with monstrance and host under a canopy while girls carried baskets of flowers.

Hope Scott was a patron of St Margaret's Ursuline Convent in Edinburgh, where two daughters and his second wife were laid to rest in the crypt. The architect George Goldie who designed Our Lady of the Angels at Mingarry was also responsible for the convent's Lady Chapel. He drew up plans for scores of Catholic churches during the Victorian era, at least seventeen of them in Scotland. The Church of Our Lady and St Andrew at Galashiels was raised two years after Goldie's only Highland venture, again paid for by James Hope Scott. The death of his second wife caused him to sell the estate to Lord Howard of Glossop, a Catholic from an old English recusant family, and withdraw from public life. His coffin joined hers at St Margaret's in that same year of 1871.

OUR LADY AND THE ANGELS, MINGARRY

Two of George Goldie's architectural plans for Mingarry can be consulted in the form of illustrations by his employer in attractive pale colours. They adorn a brochure compiled by Jean Lawson to celebrate 150 years. Modestly she chose not to identify herself by name or by that of her husband Patrick Stephen-Samuels. He leads the music. Jean has drawn on the memories of older members of the congregation as well as consulting a wide range of documentary sources, and the result is an excellent production which ought to be known to many. Her work, freely shared, has proved most helpful on the earlier chapels of Moidart.

The brochure includes a 600-word account of the first Mass celebrated by Bishop Murdoch on the Feast of the Guardian Angels, 2 October 1862. The weather turning unexpectedly dry, a procession round the outer walls (sun-wise according to ancient ways?) was held to bless them. Father Ireland's *Some Priests of Moidart* carries the complete press report from the Oban Times, a weekly which began in the previous year. Details of the structure on a north-south axis bear repeating here: 'It consists of a single aisle, the chancel being in the form of an apse at one end, and contains 450 sittings. The stone used in the building is almost entirely a handsome grey granite found on the spot, but the wooden fittings, benches, etc., which were particularly admired, were brought by the contractor ready-made from London.' This was a Mr Simpson of Tottenham Court Road: George Goldie's office was no doubt somewhere in the vicinity. The reporter admitted to a lack of familiarity with the language in stating that 'what appeared, at least, to be a most eloquent sermon in Gaelic' was given by the Rev. William McIntosh of Arisaig. There are fewer 'sittings' nowadays as the rear of the church has been turned into a social area for refreshments.

Hope Scott generously supplied £2,600 for the church and presbytery, but there were problems from the start. The site was an exposed one and the enormous roof was heavy, so that upright beams bolted through the main walls had to be added. Stained glass windows on the south wall celebrate St Columba and St Finnan. They are not mentioned in the press report but were probably installed in the Hope Scott era. Almost certainly of that time is a chancel window to St Hyacinth. The family property of Woodchester in the Cotswolds had a Dominican priory, and Jean Lawson speculates – quite plausibly – that there may have been a family

TILED ALTAR, MINGARRY

devotion to this far-travelled Blackfriar. Her further speculations on the building come from thorough familiarity with it:

'[Hope Scott] evidently decided, after Goldie drew the first plans, to add an "Organ Chamber" which necessitated a second, less detailed, plan. There are no signs now of the Chamber's original use. It became a Lady Chapel and later, in the 1980s, was partitioned off to form a confessional and a small room now used as a general side chapel. The original plan shows the confessional as being served from the sacristy. A parishioner has memories of an organ at the back of the church before one was installed in its present site.'

That is below the Gospel side of the altar where Jean's husband plays the organ. Further on altars: 'The turning of the altar so that the priest would face the congregation brought about the destruction of the very ornate and, to many, beautifully tiled altar. It was possibly not to the taste of the time but in a dark chancel, before the skylights and with the only windows tucked out of sight of the nave, the altar must have provided a wonderful focus. Today it can be regretted that it was not left in place behind the new altar, even if covered over.' Canon Iain Gillies, whose carpentry at Arisaig and Knoydart has been noted, carved the new altar's Chi-rho – the first two letters of Christ in Greek.

☧

12 - BOTH ENDS OF LOCH SHIEL

St Finnan's Isle or *Eilean Fhianain* at the south-west end of Loch Shiel offers a suitable start to this final chapter. Several people have discussed it in print, but pride of place goes to Hugh Cheape. Formerly the Museum of Scotland's expert in Edinburgh on all things Highland, he is now a professor at the Gaelic College of *Sabhal Mòr Ostaig* in Skye. He has local connections as owner of the Glenaladale estate further up the loch with a house at the end of it. In the magazine *Lochaber Life* he wrote 'St Finnan the Apostle of Moidart'.

As with other Celtic saints there is uncertainty about the meaning of the name (perhaps 'Little Fair One') and also in which of three possible centuries he left Ireland. Finnan may have come from the kingdom of Dalriada in Antrim or possibly Donegal. In Scotland local tradition helps a little, and his movements are suggested by place-names. Dedications to St Finnan in the islands of Islay, Mull, Muck, Coll and Tiree imply a route towards mainland Ardnamurchan: 'After landing from his boat, St Finnan proceeded inland towards the north side of the peninsula, probably following a natural route to the west of Ben Hiant (*Beinn Shianta*, the "Sacred Mountain") over to the Achateny Water and Kilmory, and turning along the coast to Swordle. He stopped to rest on the shoulder of a hill between the townships of Ockle and Gortenfern, and from this point, known as *Suidhe Fhíanain* or St Finnan's Seat, he saw inland more than ten miles to the east the island which now commemorates his name.'

The verdant Green Isle, *An t-Eilean Uaine*, would have stood out then as now against dark loch and dun hillsides. It is presumed that the saint made a cell for himself on it. However the Celtic bell with its chain is of later date, the altar on which it rests much later still – perhaps sixteenth century. A further century on saw the bell removed and then recovered minus its clapper, since replaced. Different stories surround the event. Alastair Cameron (who wrote as North Argyll) identified the recovering caretaker as *Niall Mòr an Eilean* whose croft on the Moidart shore, which he held rent free of Clanranald, is still called *Croit an Eilean*. Well into Victorian times the bell was being carried *deisal* or sun-wise round the island as in days of old.

In her *Further Wanderings – Mainly in Argyll* M. E. M. Donaldson was rhapsodic: 'In early summer the island, now the home of blackcock, is ablaze with broom, which makes it a remarkable sight, setting off the grey buildings very effectively, and along its shores are many waders and numerous greenshank. Landing at the little pier, and climbing up the slopes of the island through the long rank grass, you will find the remains of the larger building, the church, 70 ft. by 17 ft.. This, shewing no structural division between nave and chancel, nor any other feature, is of no architectural interest whatever. But within, there is the greatest interest in the ancient altar, surrounded, indeed, by a thick bed of nettles,

GRAVES ON THE GREEN ISLE

but still in its place at the east end, above it having been set in modern times an old weather-worn stone crucifix. Upon the *mensa* of the altar itself stands the Bell of St Finnan, one of the seven quadrangular Celtic bells remaining in Scotland. This is of bronze, and has a most beautiful note as you can discover for yourself by taking it up and ringing it.'

Father Charles MacDonald (who must have buried many on the island) blamed three Protestant Clanranald chiefs for letting the chapel fall into disrepair. The custom of making an annual pilgrimage on the feast of the patron saint died out to the extent that no one remembered the month far less the day. One custom which survived through post-Reformation centuries was the burial of Protestants from Argyll on that side of the island, while Catholics were interred on the Moidart side. Father Charles identified a Donald MacVarish from Mingarry as the man who carved the rude stone crosses in one corner. He had died about fifty years before.

Although the vegetation is now a constant matter of concern it was kept under reasonable control in Lord Glossop's time. This landlord who died in 1883 provided a funeral boat large enough to convey both coffin and mourners but it did not long outlast him. Used for other purposes, exposed to all weathers, it was finally broken up. Fourteen years later, following a particularly dangerous crossing in a small vessel, local people formed a ferry boat committee with an appeal for money made through the *Oban Times*. Among those approached directly was the second Lord Glossop. The young man, who had not been consulted in advance, shocked the committee with a veto on the grounds that his tenant at Dalilea had been given responsibility for crossings. Money was returned to collectors.

Widow Ada MacVicar wrote the heir a soothing letter from Kinlochmoidart: 'The first cause of the people wishing for another arrangement for the Eilean Finnan ferry was that the funeral held at E. Finnan last Jan. was held at risk of life crossing to the burial island. . . It took six men with four oars two hours to cross. The boat could only take on board, in addition to the coffin, barely enough men to carry it to its resting place – the others could not be taken over.' In due course his lordship provided a suitable boat and boat-house at Dalilea. Jean Lawson gave a talk on all this to the Moidart Heritage Group, adding a postscript to the effect that after the Glossop era two successive owners refused permission for a pilgrimage to the Green Isle. There has been at least one in recent times when Fr John Angus MacDonald, then of Fort William, said Mass there in September 2002.

Iain Thornber is involved in a long-term project to map graves and identify as many as possible of those buried on the island. There is for example a very fine Celtic cross to commemorate Fr Charles MacDonald. Archie Rhu

MacDonald as owner of the Lochshiel estate was brought there for reburial. The father of the famous Gaelic poet Alasdair MacMaighstir Alasdair lies under a flat stone with a skeleton carved on it. In his lifetime Master Alasdair MacDonald was renowned for walking thirty miles to and from Dalilea to hold an Episcopalian service at Kilmory in Ardnamurchan. There was no need to name him. Instead the grave stone carries lines from Revelations XIV V: 'And I heard a voice saying unto me, Write, Blessed are the dead which die in the Lord from henceforth. Yea saith the Spirit, that they may rest from their labours; and their works do follow them.'

In the spirit of inquiry Iain made notes on a 1981 funeral at the Glenuig chapel conducted by Fr Joseph McShane. The lengthy preaching was 'almost evangelical', the singing poor by Church of Scotland standards. (An American author has written a book about *Why Catholics Don't Sing*.) At the end of the service a young piper – probably one of the three Glenuig MacDonald brothers who grew up to become excellent performers – played *Mo Dachaidh* ('My Home') as the coffin was carried to a hearse outside the Glenuig Inn. Cars followed to Dalilea where the coffin was placed athwart a boat, four men steadying it as wreaths were put aboard. Thanks to an outboard motor, they no longer had to row.

The late Donald Kennedy's widow and sister followed in a second boat with other mourners. When more men landed his coffin was carried up the hill, women going ahead with the wreaths. The boats went back and forward till everyone was across. There was a short Bible reading at the graveside and then a prayer for the faithful departed. The piper played 'Flowers of the Forest' and saluted the chief mourners. The grave-digger, gamekeeper Hugh MacDonald from Moss, held a spade with earth out to the priest who led the way in dropping a handful of earth on the coffin. The grave was then filled in by male mourners taking turns with the spade, while women said prayers at the graves of their relations. Quite a few knelt at the tomb of Fr Jerome Ireland who had died seven years before.

The grave-digger told Iain Thornber that the large roughly hewn stone crosses came from the north-east Sunart side of the loch and the tradition was that they had been

ALTAR, THE GREEN ISLE

dragged to the water side on birch branches. The company were ferried back to the Moidart side and a crate of whisky was produced from the chief mourner's car. Women as well as men took drams, but the drinking ceased, at least temporarily, when Fr McShane (who did not drink) started his car and drove off to Mingarry. This provided a signal for the mourners to disperse.

*

At the other end of the loch the 1815 Glenfinnan Monument commemorates the raising of the Stuart standard sixty years earlier. In a well researched paper Neil Cameron examined the role of Clanranald's rakehell companion Alexander MacDonald of Glenaladale who died, aged twenty-eight, at the start of the year in which his monument was built. It was the work of James Gillespie Graham who designed the Edinburgh chapel where the French Marshal MacDonald had last taken part in Sunday worship. His travel diary provides fresh information which has still to be acknowledged. At that time the tower was entered by way of a two-storey extension: the geologist John MacCulloch compared the building to 'a carpenter's mallet with the handle uppermost'. The extension was soon to be removed leaving the familiar tower. Another MacCulloch called it a 'shooting-box'; for Neil Cameron it was 'evidently a bothy'. Whatever else the building may have been or become, credence must be given to Marshal MacDonald who would either have been told at the inn or by his guide the well-informed MacDonald of Staffa. The diary for 28 June records that 'close to the shore, a small chapel has been built and, next to it, a round tower which is tall and crenellated around its top.' In the previous year work had been commissioned by John Macdonald of Borrodale, who fell heir to his cousin Archie Rhu's already leaking structure, to provide new floors for the two rooms along with window frames and shutters – lath and plaster upstairs and down. Entry to the room above was from the whitewashed spiral staircase in the tower. It was common enough at this time for chapels to have accommodation for priests on an upper floor, and no doubt the Rev. James MacGregor (who served Glenfinnan from Fort William) was grateful during his overnight stays for the fireplace installed in 1824.

Arisaig's Vicar General William McIntosh had disapproved of the Moidart priest Ranald Rankin's plans for 'centrical' chapel. He also opposed the younger man on how the upper end of Loch Shiel should be served. Rankin had addressed the challenge presented by Austin MacDonald many years before that 'if there was a resident priest, such as I cannot be, in a short time all the neighbouring district would return to the Catholic faith.' But the willingness of people to gather near an inn gave McIntosh concern: 'Mr Rankin on coming to his new mission being full of zeal, and finding a considerable number of people, from various motives no doubt, attend divine service the first Sunday or two he officiated at Glenfinnan . . . commenced going every eight weeks, and he now finds this heavy on his hand and is anxious to get rid of it altogether; hence he is pressing me to get Glenfinnan attached to Fort William as it was originally.'

*

In 1844 the Scottish Catholic Directory reported that the Rev. Archibald Chisholm visited Glenfinnan occasionally using an upstairs room in a private house for the services. A chapel was 'much wanted' as the room was too small for the congregation. Donald MacDonald, youngest son of the Glenaladale family, was ordained in the same year. He had received his preparation for priesthood at St Cuthbert's College, Ushaw, near Durham. A sickly youth, he was 'ordained to die' according to Tearlach MacFarlane, owner of the Glenfinnan Hotel. He recovered sufficiently to act as chaplain to the family and was 'at Borrodale with no duties 1858-62'. We know there was a domestic chapel because its altar was passed on to Glenuig. Eleven years later, his brother Angus having extended Glenfinnan House (now Hotel) and moved from Borrodale, a very fine church was opened at the head of Loch Shiel. Angus MacDonald of Glenaladale was buried in the church soon after the foundations were laid in January 1872.

The architect was Edward Welby Pugin, oldest son of Augustus Welby Pugin of Gothic Revival fame. The younger Pugin's 'style and plans became normative for Roman Catholic churches in the British Isles in the second half of the nineteenth century.' There is no reason to suppose that Pugin visited the district to approve the magnificent setting above Loch Shiel - St Mary's, Haddington, was one of his few other

GLENFINNAN CHURCH

Scottish projects. Father Donald's nephew Colonel John A. MacDonald of Glenaladale put up the money. As the walls rose Fr Donald's pastoral work went on record for the first time: 'On Sundays and Holidays Mass at 11; also Stations of the Cross, Benediction, and Instructions in Christian Doctrine. On Week-days Mass at 81/2.' All this took place in a ground floor room at Glenfinnan House. The priest's room was in the tower above the front entrance.

The church being built incorporated a rich variety of stone: blue native granite marbled with quartz for the ashlar

THE ROSE WINDOW, GLENFINNAN

work, cream granite for the buttresses, and light pink Elgin granite for the edging of doors and windows. According to local tradition the granite came from the Rubislaw quarry in Aberdeen via the canal to Corpach, and thence by horse and cart to the site. Two years under construction, the interior has been characterised as 'a light and airy space of considerable grandeur. The nave is fully aisled and rises to a clearstory.' Three pillars on each side of the centre aisle with arches between add Gothic dignity. The church of St Mary and St Finnan was dedicated on 19 August 1873 by Archbishop Charles Eyre who presided over the Western District from Glasgow. He had been a fellow student of Donald MacDonald at Ushaw, and two other English bishops were there to strengthen the connection with Durham. The Stuart standard had been raised on 19 August 1745, and a set of bagpipes played then were again brought into use as the congregation left.

Father Angus MacDonald, nephew of the Glenfinnan priest, had been ordained at Ushaw in the year before this opening and was a curate in the Anderston district of Glasgow. Three years after the church (never a chapel) was dedicated at the head of Loch Shiel Fr Angus took charge of the Arisaig mission which included Borrodale where he was born. His time there was short. At the restoration of the Episcopal Hierarchy in 1878 he went to Oban as Bishop of Argyll and the Isles, having been consecrated by Archbishop Eyre. In 1892 he was translated to become Archbishop of St Andrews and Edinburgh. He died in the first year of the new century at the age of sixty-six. His once sickly uncle had lived and worked at Glenfinnan into his eighties.

The priests who followed are well described in a brief history of the parish by John Watts which can be consulted online. Dr Watts was well placed for the task, having edited a modern edition of *Moidart; or Among the Clanranalds* and added useful notes. Going some way beyond Moidart, the brief history describes how a majority of the congregation lived on both sides of Loch Eil. Nearly half way through his twenty-two years at Glenfinnan Fr Patrick O'Regan came to an agreement with Francis Cameron-Head whereby a prefabricated wooden hut was made available for worship. Joseph MacLeod offered land on his croft on the road to Fort William. Volunteers cleared the site, dismantled the hut at Inverailort and re-assembled what was to be the last of the wider district's chapels at Alltdarroch. It opened on 9 June 1950, the feast of St Columba, and thereafter Sunday Mass (previously held occasionally in Lochiel School) became available on a weekly basis.

BELL AND CHURCH, GLENFINNAN

The church of St Mary and St Finnan is a wonderful building. One of its wonders which catches the eye of passers by is a very large bell suspended near ground level. The money ran out before a belfry tower could be raised: the door leading to the intended tower is still in evidence. On the bell is inscribed a tribute to one of the most beautiful views in the Highlands:

Benedicite montes et colles
Mare et flumina Domine.

'May the mountains, the hills, the sea and the loch bless the Lord.' Another wonder, dating from as recently as 1995, has to be viewed from inside the church. It is a large rose window behind the altar which was designed by Fr Calum MacNeill and installed by Ormsby of Scarisbrick in Catholic Lancashire.

Father Donald MacDonald cost the diocese nothing, living as he did in Glenfinnan House with financial support from the family. When the first of seventeen priests succeeded him there was no presbytery. As the years went by the weather in one of the wettest parts of Scotland had its effect on the fabric. Father O'Regan wrote to his bishop in Oban about 'hearing the damp and green walls saying to me, "'Tis your job to dry us."' The house ceased to be a problem after Glenfinnan began to be served by Canon Terry driving round on the new road from Mingarry. Restoring and drying out the roof and walls was attempted in a major refurbishment thirty years ago but still the paint peeled away. The congregation was never large, money was always short, and it must be hoped that help from the wider public will be available (as it has been from Canadian MacDonalds) following the latest thorough renewal begun in 2013 and completed two years later.

John Watts has featured in this final chapter. In the same year of 2013 a book of his came out under the title *A Record of a Generous People,* a history of the Catholic Church in Argyll & the Isles. Let him have the last word: 'In August 1873 Archbishop Eyre visited the West Highlands to open the new church in Glenfinnan. It seems strange that the district had not had a parish until now. It was strategically placed, standing sentinel at the eastern border of the lands of Clanranald. . . If it was long in coming it had been worth the wait. Designed by the renowned architect Edward Welby Pugin in the "late Early English" style, its elegance of line was enhanced by the use of a variety of stone. . . Architecture, natural beauty and history combined to make SS Mary & Finnan what it remains today – one of Highland Catholicism's most memorable and iconic churches.'

Further Reading

Odo Blundell, *The Catholic Highlands of Scotland: The Western Highlands and Islands* (Edinburgh, 1917).

M. E. M. Donaldson, *Wanderings in the Western Highlands and Islands, recounting Highland and Clan History, traditions, archaeology, literature and folklore.* (Paisley, 1923, 1927).

John Dye (ed.), *Some Priests of Moidart*. From the weekly bulletins of Fr Jerome Ireland, available from Moidart Heritage Group's History Hut, Glenuig.

Paul Galbraith, *Blessed Morar (Morair Bheannaichte).* Centenary of Our Lady and St Cumin's, 1989, available at church.

Jean Lawson, *Our Lady of the Angels, Mingarry, 1862-2012.* Sesquicentenary of Moidart's principal church, 2012. Available History Hut, Glenuig.

Rev. Charles MacDonald, *Moidart; or Among the Clanranalds* (Edinburgh, 1989). Centennial edition with new material by Iain Thornber.

Elizabeth MacDonald, *The Church of Scotland in Arisaig, Parish of North West Lochaber* (Arisaig, 2011).

Brian Murray, *Yes, No, Maybe: A Death in Kylesmorar in 1830.* Privately published, available through Mallaig Heritage Centre.

Timothy Neat, *When I Was Young: Voices from Lost Communities in Scotland. The Islands* (Edinburgh, Birlinn, 2000).

Alasdair Roberts, 'William McIntosh: an untypical link between East and West Highland Catholicism', *Innes Review*, 42 (1991), 137-42.

'Roman Catholicism in the Highlands', James Kirk (ed.), *The Church in the Highlands* (Edinburgh, 1999), 63-88.

'William McIntosh in the West Highlands: changing the practice of religion', *Innes Review*, 54 (2003), 111-41.

'Whisky and priests in the Highlands', *Northern Scotland*, 24 (2004), 17-44.

'Education and faith in the Catholic Highlands of Scotland', *Recusant History*, 27 (2005), 537-58.

'Dom Odo Blundell OSB (1868-1943): a different kind of historian', *Innes Review*, 56 (2005), 14-45, with Br. Paschal Downs OSB.

Tales of the Morar Highlands (Edinburgh: Birlinn, 2006, 2011).

Review article 'John Watts in the Highlands', *Innes Review* 60 (2009), 69-81.

Review article '*The French MacDonald*: Catholic connections', *Innes Review* 62 (2011), 82-7.

Jacobite Traitor? Coll MacDonell and the Prince (Prestonpans: Prestoungrange and Cuthill Press, 2013) with Valerie Cameron Smith.

'Coll MacColl (1787-1842): Son of the Manse and Highland Priest', *West Highland Notes & Queries*, 3, 26 (October 2014), 13-23.

Denis Rixson, *Arisaig and Morar: A History* (Edinburgh: Birlinn, 2002)

Knoydart: A History (Edinburgh: Birlinn, 2011).

Iain Thornber, *The Cameron Collection: Moidart & Arisaig in the 19th Century.* (Fort William, 2007).

John Watts (ed.), *Moidart; or Among the Clanranalds* (Edinburgh: Birlinn, 1996).

Hugh MacDonald: Highlander, Jacobite, Bishop (East Linton: John Donald, 2004).

A Record of a Generous People: A History of the Catholic Church in Argyll & the Isles (Glasgow: Mungo Press, 2013).

Wendy Wood, *Moidart and Morar* (Edinburgh, 1950)

Index